WESTBOURNE LIBR
ALUM CHINE ROAD
BOURNEMOUTH BH4 8DX
Tel: 01202 761845

P

19. SEP 06

BOURNEMOUTH LIBRARIES

610654201 P

For Julie, also a fighter

Pankhurst

Jad Adams

BOURNEMOUTH

2005

LIBRARIES

HAUS PUBLISHING · LONDON

First published in Great Britain in 2003 by
Haus Publishing Limited
26 Cadogan Court, Draycott Avenue
London SW3 3BX

Copyright © Jad Adams, 2003

The moral rights of the author have been asserted.

A CIP catalogue record for this book is available from the British Library

ISBN 1-904341-53-5

Designed and typeset in Garamond by
Palimpsest Book Production Limited, Polmont, Stirlingshire

Printed and bound by Graphicom in Vicenza, Italy

Front cover: Emmeline Pankhurst. Topham Picturepoint
Back cover: Emmeline Pankhurst. Ann Ronan Picture Library

CONDITIONS OF SALE

All rights reserved. No part of this publication may be reproduced, stored in
a retrieval system, or transmitted in any form or by any means, electronic,
mechanical, photocopying, recording or otherwise, without the prior
permission of the publisher.

This book is sold subject to the condition that it shall not, by way of trade
or otherwise, be lent, re-sold, hired out or otherwise circulated without the
publisher's prior consent in any form of binding or cover other than that in
which it is published and without a similar condition including this
condition being imposed on the subsequent purchaser

Contents

Introduction

There has been no more paradoxical figure in British politics than Emmeline Pankhurst. A century after the foundation of her Women's Social and Political Union dispute still rages between her supporters and detractors over the most basic questions: what did she achieve? Was her activity a positive or a negative force in the struggle to secure the vote for women? Was she a courageous, self-sacrificing martyr or a sour widow dominating her movement as much as her family? Did she have a clear, principled vision or was she a self-seeking opportunist?

For her most fervent admirers no praise could be higher: she was the saintly leader willing to suffer torment to the point of death for the cause. To her critics she was a narrow-minded autocrat who led young women into dire physical danger in a ruthless desire to gain the franchise only on her own terms.

Emmeline Pankhurst was a well brought up woman, a person of middle-class morals, dress and tastes who could, however, still declare to a public meeting, *We have blown up the Chancellor's house!*[1] For more than two years, from March 1912, sabotage tore across the country in the name of Votes for Women. Historic houses and churches were burned and bombed, paintings slashed, and water mains, telegraph cables, sporting venues and letter boxes damaged. Hundreds of women were imprisoned for the cause. Many underwent hunger-strikes and forcible feeding. Emmeline Pankhurst led from the front, undertaking not only repeated hunger strikes but also the more serious hunger and thirst strikes.

Emmeline did not chain herself to railings or disrupt any sporting events, nor did she undergo forcible feeding, though she came to personify the suffrage campaign to such an extent that it was, and is, popularly assumed that she did all these. In fact she did not even originate any of the violent actions, from window-smashing to arson, undertaken by suffragettes. But she embraced and encouraged those activities that had the greatest publicity value. Her genius was to realise how far women would go in pursuit of the franchise and to encourage them to test their personal limits. She made individual sacrifice collective and the resulting collective struggle into a great theatrical public representation of Everywoman's fight for justice.

The suffragettes' destructive phase covered only a small part of Emmeline Pankhurst's agitation for the vote, which started when she attended her first suffrage campaign meeting as a girl in 1872 and ended in 1914 when the policy of militancy was called off. Until 1909 even 'militant' actions were symbolic rather than actually violent. There was a militant truce for most of 1910 and 1911.

In the first five years of its existence the Women's Social and Political Union, founded in Emmeline's house in a suburb of Manchester in 1903, had grown through the power of word and organisation into one of the most successful pressure groups in history. In 1908, Emmeline addressed the largest ever indoor meeting on women's suffrage, at the Albert Hall; and that year the WSPU organised Women's Sunday in Hyde Park, one of the largest ever demonstrations for any cause. Emmeline was responsible for promoting this radical cause with high emotion when the time was right for it and for choosing to work with such brilliant organisers as the Pethick Lawrences, who set the pace for the growth of the movement before Emmeline had them expelled.

She was an odd leader for a movement calling for more democracy. The WSPU was dominated by Emmeline and ruled by her and her family members. When a group of supporters urged her to behave less autocratically, she obliged them to leave. Even her daughter Sylvia was expelled for doctrinal failings and another daughter, Adela, was sent to Australia.

The strongest trait in Emmeline's emotional makeup was courage, but it was closely followed by the confidence that everything she did was right and any alternatives wrong. Yet, in spite of such indomitable certainty, she was a radical Liberal in early life, then a socialist, then leader of her own Women's Party, and ended her days as a candidate for the Conservatives. She held every political belief with the same unshakeable conviction, until the next supplanted it.

She recognised the vote as an important symbolic objective in the fight for women's equality, but was most committed to the changes she believed enfranchised women could make in society, particularly in the field of sex crime, which she dwelt upon to enrich her speeches. She wanted the vote to be given to women on the same basis as to men, but her views on what women could achieve in politics were not based on equality. She repeatedly insisted that women would do better than men in the political sphere. Like her opponents, she saw the sexes as different, but giving woman, not man, superiority.

The suffrage campaign was Emmeline Pankhurst's major life work, but far from her only public activity. She successfully campaigned in Manchester for free speech when the council tried to suppress it. She was at different times a Poor Law Guardian and a member of the School Board, and was for nine years in a paid post as a Registrar of Births and Deaths, which maintained her contact with the lives of the poor. She applied a great deal of her prodigious determination to fruitless attempts to become a successful shopkeeper, an endeavour which a less tenacious woman would have abandoned long before. She was engaged in patriotic and anti-Bolshevik propaganda during the First World War and the years after in the United States and Canada. In Canada she also campaigned for the National Council for Combating Venereal Disease.

Emmeline was also a wife and mother. As soon as the suffrage story commences one is thrown into the psychodrama of the

Pankhurst family: her husband Richard's principled obstinacy, her daughter Christabel's vanity, Adela's isolation, Sylvia's self-sacrifice and, always presiding over this, Emmeline's determination to succeed. While her story has to be theirs also, and the Pankhursts were all interesting people, none of the family would have been more than local heroes on their own. Emmeline was the star and the driving force. The exiled Adela gave one of the most penetrating critiques of her mother when she said: 'It was the family attitude – Cause First and human relations – nowhere . . . if [Emmeline] had been tolerant and broadminded, she would not have been the leader of the suffragettes.'[2]

Girl to Wife: 1858–1879

Everything about Emmeline Pankhurst is controversial, even her date of birth. She always celebrated her birthday on 14 July 1858, the anniversary of the storming of the Bastille in 1789, at the beginning of the French Revolution. She believed in omens and said that this auspicious birth date had an influence on her life, as if she too were destined to overthrow tyranny. It has been questioned whether this was her actual date of birth but for Emmeline, who came from a radical family and as a girl was to become entranced by French culture, Bastille Day was the chosen date.

She was the eldest girl in a family of ten surviving children born to Robert and Sophie Goulden in Moss Side, Manchester. They had family memories of the Peterloo massacre of 1819 and the Anti-Corn Law League campaign of the 1840s though, tellingly, there is no mention of the Gouldens having been involved in the Chartist movement (the campaign for universal male suffrage). They were radicals, and there can be no doubt that families such as theirs wanted life to be better for everyone, but first in the queue for that betterment were to be the industrious middle class. Robert Goulden was so successful he became a partner in and manager of a cotton printing and bleach works at Seedley. Emmeline largely grew up in the family home of Seedley Cottage with holidays at the family's other house on the Isle of Man. She learned to play the piano and her father was keen on amateur dramatics so performance was always part of family life, as was the partisan drama of elections, in which the children played what part they could when their family supported Liberal candidates.

Emmeline was an alert, clever child and a precocious reader, particularly of romance and adventure. *The Pilgrim's Progress*, the *Odyssey*, Thomas Carlyle's *French Revolution* and Harriet Beecher Stowe's *Uncle Tom's Cabin* were particular favourites. Her mother was a keen abolitionist and Emmeline's earliest political memory was of collecting money in a bag at a bazaar to relieve the poverty of newly emancipated slaves in America. Sophie Goulden subscribed to *Women's Suffrage Journal* and both parents were supporters of equal suffrage for men and women. Emmeline was to consider this an absolute principle, causing endless dispute with other suffrage society leaders who were prepared to accept a more limited female suffrage as an interim measure.

Emmeline later remembered how her home welcomed the Reform Act of 1867, which enfranchised many working class and middle-income men. During the debate over the Act in the House of Commons, John Stuart Mill proposed the enfranchisement of women. Though the motion was defeated by 194 votes to 73, the large minority already willing to support it showed the direction in which the political wind was blowing. Two years earlier the Conservative leader Disraeli had declared himself in favour of women's suffrage. Emmeline attended her first women's suffrage meeting when she was fourteen in 1872, hearing Lydia Becker, secretary for the Manchester National Union for Women's Suffrage.

Emmeline spoke of her childhood as *protected by love and a comfortable* home but felt instinctively that *there was something lacking . . . some false conception of family relations, some incomplete ideal.* Even as she received the basic education offered to middle-class girls, Emmeline's radical sense led her to question the facts of her own existence. *It used to puzzle me to understand why I was under such a particular obligation to make home attractive to my brothers. We were on excellent terms of friendship, but it was never suggested to them as a duty that they make home attractive to me.*[3] As Emmeline knew very well by the time she made these remarks, boys were not groomed to do housework: they were groomed to provide houses in which such activity could take place. With social restrictions on women in the workplace, it could not be otherwise. Emmeline was rebelling against the assumption of innate male superiority and women's acquiescence from an early age.

Emmeline (second right) with the Rocheforts in Geneva, 1875. Her friend Noemie is on the far left

At 14 years of age, Emmeline was sent to the École Normale de Neuilly in France by her parents who wanted her to become an accomplished lady but also wanted her to have a rounded education that showed her more of the world than Manchester could provide. When she arrived there in 1872, Paris had within the year experienced defeat in the Franco-Prussian War and the brutal suppression of the Commune uprising. She quickly fell under the spell of France, particularly through her friendship with Noémie Rochefort, daughter of a communard, Henri Rochefort, currently in exile, tales of whose romantic exploits thrilled Emmeline. Living in Paris under Prussian occupation gave Emmeline a life-long prejudice against all things German.

She returned to Manchester at 18, graceful and confident as her parents had hoped she would be, and with a fine dress sense, which never left her. Her daughter Sylvia describes her as having at this time: 'a slender svelte figure, raven black hair, an olive skin with a slight flush of red in the cheeks, delicately pencilled black eyebrows, beautiful expressive eyes of an unusually deep violet blue, above all a magnificent carriage and a voice of remarkable melody'.[4]

Emmeline in 1879

Emmeline soon returned to France, taking her sister Mary with her. Noémie was now married to a painter, and she wanted Emmeline to live nearby so they could be cultured hostesses together. In order to achieve this, Emmeline needed a household and would have to marry. Noémie introduced her to a suitor, a writer of some distinction who would take Emmeline if she came with a dowry. Emmeline liked this idea and proposed it to her father, who did not. Robert Goulden would not sell his daughter in the marriage market, and he ordered both girls back, doubtless now realising that the liberation of a foreign education also had its disadvantages. Emmeline's suitor had no interest in her with no dowry and withdrew his offer of marriage. Emmeline perversely blamed her father for the loss of this man and of her sophisticated career as a Parisian hostess.

A much more appropriate match was the brilliant radical lawyer Richard Pankhurst who was 44 in 1878 when Emmeline, newly returned from Paris, first saw him addressing a meeting opposing the jingoism of those who wanted to confront Russia militarily over the Balkan crisis. A religious nonconformist, he had been educated at Owens College (later Manchester University) and the University of London where he became a Doctor of Law. He was called to the Bar in 1867 and later worked as a barrister in Manchester where he was known as 'the Red Doctor', a play on his left-wing views (he was on the far left of the Liberal party) and his great red beard. He was not a physically impressive man – he was below average height and had a high-pitched voice – but he was a republican, anti-imperialist and an active advocate of women's suffrage. He had drafted the first statute specifically about women's franchise, the Women's Disabilities Removal Bill, which received its second reading by a majority of 33 but was then killed by Gladstone's personal opposition. Pankhurst was almost all Emmeline could want, and luckily for her he was single. He had decided to remain so to devote himself to the cause.

Emmeline Pankhurst was born into and thrived in the Age of Reform, the century in which first the middle class then the working class was the force for change. The vote was extended to men of the middle class in 1832, large numbers of the urban working class in 1867 and agricultural workers in 1884. Constitutional battles were fought to permit Catholics, nonconformists, Jews and finally atheists to sit in the House of Commons. In 1846, the middle class, generally supporters of the Liberal party, had secured a victory over the landed aristocracy with the repeal of the Corn Laws, which had imposed an import tariff on foreign grain, and henceforth their ideas of progress dominated the political scene. The Manchester into which Emmeline was born was dedicated to free trade and the principle that business should be free from government interference. Within this Liberal ascendancy, and often working contrary to it, was a group of high-minded radicals such as Richard Pankhurst, dedicated to such principles as internationalism, republicanism and female emancipation.

Emmeline thought Dr Pankhurst would regard her as an ill-educated child, but he was entranced by his young admirer. He had also seen her or had been made aware of her interest, and he decided to pay court to her in the manner of their type: he wrote to invite her to become involved in a movement for the higher education of women. Before the end of September he was writing to her as 'Dearest Treasure' and pledging the hope that in their life together, 'Every struggling cause shall be ours.'[5]

Richard Marsden Pankhurst in 1879, the year of his marriage to Emmeline

Emmeline was so passionate to fling herself into the cause that she proposed a 'free union': that they should have their love legitimised by no ceremony but should live together as a free man and woman, proposing that they should 'manifest both their independence of spirit and their solidarity with the sufferings of unhappy wives'.[6]

Pankhurst knew, however, that such an agreement was not a matter of private arrangement alone: strong women in free unions such as George Eliot and the feminist Elizabeth Wolstenholme had suffered calumny and social ostracism that had detracted from their work. Richard's tactics demonstrated how he had the measure of Emmeline: if he had told her they had to marry or society would gossip she would have petulantly refused to marry; instead, he told her that marriage was for the good of the cause, and she jumped into it with alacrity. Still, she teased him with: *Wouldn't you have liked to try first how we should get on?*[7]

Richard Pankhurst lived with his parents but his father had recently died. When his mother died while the couple were making their wedding plans they did not, as might be expected, choose to wait a few months between the funeral and the wedding feast. Richard was suffering agonies of grief alone in his empty house and Emmeline felt it necessary to support him for fear he would break down under the weight of bereavement and his heavy workload.

The wedding was duly brought forward and took place on 18 December 1879 at St Luke's Weaste, Lancashire. Robert Goulden was still, however, not prepared to settle a dowry on his eldest daughter, a decision that never ceased to anger her.

Every Struggling Cause: 1879–1898

The accelerated wedding arrangements meant Sophie Goulden had no time for the quiet talk which mothers had with their daughters to inform erstwhile innocent girls about the sex act. She went to Emmeline's room the night before the wedding and said, 'I want to talk to you.' Emmeline replied: *I do not want to listen*, which has been interpreted as meaning she did not want to cast a shadow over the beauty of her courtship. She almost certainly had some idea what her mother was going to say, having spent four years in France where attitudes towards sex were somewhat more rational than in Victorian Manchester. She was also perhaps irritated that her mother had waited so long before giving a daughter essential instruction.[8]

The couple wasted no time in starting a family. Nine calendar months after the wedding, on 22 September 1880, Christabel Harriette was born in their home in Drayton Terrace, Old Trafford, Manchester. Estelle Sylvia (always known as Sylvia) was born on 5 May 1882; Francis Henry (known as 'Frank') was born on 27 February 1884; and on 19 June 1885 Adela Constantia was added to the family. Emmeline suffered intensely from neuralgia during these pregnancies and from stomach complaints she was later to exacerbate with hunger strikes.

While these pregnancies were taking place, the young couple had financial and political difficulties and their relationship with Robert Goulden was tense. Richard Pankhurst was more successful as a political figure than as a barrister and so the Pankhursts moved into the Goulden household at Seedley. Emmeline had hoped her father would settle sufficient property on her so that she and Richard could dedicate themselves to political work and this move went some of the way towards allowing the cost of the Pankhurst family to rest on the Goulden family.

The cost to Robert Goulden was to be greater, however. There were deep divisions in the Manchester Liberal Party over imperialist expansion, which was generally supported by wealthy businessmen in the party, but opposed by those, such as Richard Pankhurst and Robert Goulden, who felt themselves to be more principled. When the pro-war faction ousted the prospective

Sylvia, Adela and Christabel Pankhurst c. 1890

parliamentary candidate, who was anti-war, Richard determined he would resign from the Liberal Party and himself stand as an Independent. Robert Goulden supported his son-in-law in an 1883 by-election that saw Richard head-to-head against a Conservative.

The Manchester Liberal Association told its members not to vote and even the Manchester Women's Suffrage Society would not come out in Richard's support, though Emmeline called on its leader, Lydia Becker, to plead with her. It may have been – 'as rumour persistently declared' – that the rather plain spinster Becker had held a torch for Richard Pankhurst before his marriage and the sight of the evidently pregnant and very pretty Emmeline putting his case for assistance was not conducive to his cause.[9] Rather contrary to the standard image of general implacable male opposition to female suffrage, Richard's Conservative opponent also supported the principle, and Lydia Becker felt her cause would be advanced whoever won.

Richard had such a collection of radical policies – including the nationalisation of land and abolition of the monarchy and the House of Lords – that he offered something to offend everyone, though it was perhaps his advocacy of Home Rule for Ireland that fatally ruined his chances. To Emmeline's shocked dismay, he lost by a huge margin: only 6,000 voted for him, a third of the vote received by the Conservative candidate.

Richard was now burdened with election expenses at the same time as wealthy Manchester Liberals, who felt moved to support only those who shared their politics, were boycotting his services. Robert Goulden's business was also boycotted; he never recovered from the financial losses that resulted and his health began to fail. Living with Emmeline and Richard aggravated Robert's problems. The couple tended to argue with him, particularly as they were now increasingly socialist and Richard had become an agnostic, thus offending against both his father-in-law's Liberalism and his Christianity. The atmosphere became so unbearable that in 1885 the young couple left. Mary Goulden, who, like Emmeline, resented parental domination, went with them.

Money was tight and Emmeline, never the soul of tact, again asked her father for a settlement of property which she felt she was owed. Robert Goulden said he had promised no such thing and Emmeline never spoke to her father again, nor saw her mother until both were widows. It may have been that this request for a settlement precipitated her departure from Seedley Cottage but, as always in matters of family dispute, the details are unclear.

Despite their battles with Emmeline's parents, the Pankhursts were an extremely happy family. Extant letters show continuing and openly demonstrated affection between Emmeline and Richard and the children adored their parents, albeit with differences in degree: Richard was particularly fond of his only son Frank, 'his heart's core'; Christabel was always her mother's favourite.[10] Emmeline recalled her home life as *as nearly ideal as possible in this imperfect world*.[11]

Emmeline wanted to get out of the provinces, to *London, where everyone wants to be* and she seized her chance to be the wife of a London MP when the Rotherhithe Liberal and Radical Association invited Richard to stand as their candidate in the general election of 1885.[12] Richard's mix of revolutionary change and reform was not so hard for London to take as for Manchester but the Conservative candidate smeared him as an atheist and the Irish voters did not support him. The Irish leader Charles Parnell had ordered them to oppose all Liberal candidates regardless of their individual views, in the hope of squeezing concessions out of the government. In practice this tactic merely contributed to a Conservative victory, both nationally and in Rotherhithe, where Richard lost by 3,327 votes to 2,800. The barrage, both verbal and physical, thrown at Richard enlivened the campaign and infuriated Emmeline.

The couple returned crestfallen to Manchester, but Emmeline's dream of living in London persisted. She committed the family to investing what little capital they had in a shop to sell fancy goods in the Hampstead Road, north London, above which they lived. She hoped they would make enough money for Richard to leave his legal work and concentrate on politics but Emerson and Company's goods were of too high a quality and too highly priced for the neighbourhood. No one in the family had the business sense to adjust the stock to suit the environment; Christmas 1887 was a Spartan affair for the children.

A further terrible blow to the family, not unconnected with the move to London, was the death of four-year-old Frank in September 1888. Richard was back in Manchester working on an inquiry at the time and Emmeline was accompanying him. Mary was looking after the children when the boy fell ill and called a doctor, who mistakenly diagnosed Frank's symptoms as croup. By the time the doctors realised he had diphtheria, it was too late. Emmeline rushed back from Manchester in time to see her son die. Her anxiety at the effect the news would have on Richard added to her grief. She feared he could not withstand the shock of a telegram, so she contacted her brother, Walter, to have him tell Richard face-to-face of the death of his favourite child.

Both parents were inconsolable. Emmeline could not look at Frank's picture or bear to hear his name mentioned. She in particular blamed herself: had she not chosen that dismal neighbourhood in north London with its foul drains, perhaps her boy would not have been lost. 'The doctors would have treated him very differently had she gone to them, not as a little shopkeeper, but as the wife of a distinguished lawyer.'[13] This was the grief speaking of course. The doctors misdiagnosed a common childhood illness because they were incompetent, not because they were wilfully discriminating against their patients on grounds of class. It was the Pankhursts' misfortune that their regular doctor was away.

Before the end of the year Emmeline was pregnant again, an event she interpreted as her son Frank returning to her and duly gave her new son Harry, who was born on 7 July 1889, the same names as his dead brother but in a different order. This did not make for the best psychological circumstances for his upbringing. Emmeline nearly died of a haemorrhage after giving birth to this child, which was doubtless a factor in her having no more.

Emmeline and Richard had by now rented a house on Russell Square in Bloomsbury, a more salubrious part of London, and Emmeline opened a new shop in Berners Street, still selling fancy and household goods, but to the better class of shopper who frequented Oxford Street. The couple still viewed both her shopkeeping and Richard's legal work not as ends in themselves but as a means to allow them to continue with political work – though the shop tended to be a drain on the family income.

Emmeline in particular supported the great causes of the day, including the match-girls' strike of poorly paid women in the Bryant and May factory in the East End in 1888 and was present at a 'free speech' meeting in Trafalgar Square in 1887 that the police attacked with truncheons. Richard and Emmeline took a leading place in the huge funeral procession of a man who died at the event under the hoofs of police horses.

At home in Russell Square Emmeline fulfilled her ambition to become a political hostess. A guest described her vitality: 'a living flame. As active as a bit of quicksilver, as glistening, as enticing. Emmeline Pankhurst was very beautiful. She looked like the model of Burne-Jones' pictures – slender, willowy, with the exquisite features of one of the saints of the great impressionist.'[14]

Emmeline was in her element, hosting soirées with such leading figures as Annie Besant, main organiser of the match-girls' strike, William Morris, the dockers' leaders John Burns and Tom Mann, Karl Marx's radical daughter Eleanor and her disreputable partner Edward Aveling, Dadhabai Naoroji, the first British MP of Indian descent, and Prince Kropotkin, the Russian anarchist and geographer. The Pankhursts' doors opened wide to revolutionary socialists and anarchists as much as to Fabians and figures from the radical wing of the Liberal party. These ecumenical, home-based gatherings showed Emmeline pursuing a far more open-spirited notion of progress than when she was running her own organisation on narrow, sectarian lines.

In July 1889 a small group of radicals gathered at Emmeline's house to congratulate Emmeline on Harry's birth, but quickly fell to political planning. They formed the Women's Franchise League, and immediately became part of the fractious history of the movement for women's voting rights. As so often in progressive politics, the basis of the division was the conflict between those willing to compromise to achieve a first step forward and those who could not stomach such a half-measure. The particular half-measure under consideration was legislation to give the vote to single female heads of households. The single-women's franchise fitted in with a variety of Victorian beliefs. Wives were represented by their husbands, it was argued, so had no need of the vote. By the same token, argued the moderate suffragists, women whose husbands had died or who had never married should therefore have the vote or they would be being taxed by local and national government without having a say in that government: a clear breach of the principle that there should be no taxation without representation.

The leaders of the national women's suffrage organisations, Lydia Becker and Millicent Garrett Fawcett, were prepared to support any degree of women's franchise as it would concede the principle of votes for women. The Women's Franchise League, on the other hand, insisted that married women should be included in any legislative change. Moderates like Becker and Fawcett denounced the Women's Franchise League as 'extremists'. The League in return ridiculed Becker and Fawcett's supporters as the 'spinster suffrage party'.

The campaign for the single-women's franchise was designed to slip in between the opposition's defences rather than to scale the high points of principle. Probably no one who believed in women's suffrage believed in its being forever limited to unmarried women. However, the inclusion or non-inclusion of married women in franchise bills became one of the main issues that split the women's suffrage movement and divided support for a variety of franchise measures.

The splits were of paramount importance. When MPs were polled by the franchise organisations, an absolute majority in the House of Commons, some 340 MPs, had now pledged their support for votes for women. If only the suffrage supporters would combine, some measure of women's suffrage was possible. Instead, true to their beliefs, Emmeline and her colleagues refused to support two private members' bills in 1889 as they did not enfranchise wives. They supported another that did but it made no headway and was never voted on. When Emmeline angrily cornered a supporter of her bill, R B Haldane, in the House of Commons lobby to urge him to take an inclusive franchise measure to a vote, he said it was merely a declaration of principle and could not become law for 50 years (he was out in his prediction by some 10 years).

As numerous votes in the House of Commons were to demonstrate, a majority of MPs were in favour of the women's franchise in principle. The issue became hotly debated because the precise way in which the franchise was extended was vitally important to political parties. No party wanted to take forward a measure that would create more voters for the other side. Conservatives were more sympathetic to a franchise based on the ownership of property as the relatively well-off were more likely to vote Conservative; Liberals were more sympathetic to a household franchise, which would give the vote to people renting property as well as owning it, as it would bring many more of their supporters into the fold.

Socialists were by no means all progressive in their attitudes to women. Many trade unionists were convinced that women as an electoral force would tend to be conservative. They felt working-class women's welfare was best provided for by banning women from the workplace and paying their husbands a decent wage; and they bitterly opposed enfranchising middle-class women before working men had the vote – in the late 1880s, more than 40 per cent of men had no vote. Supporters of greater democracy could honestly claim that universal manhood suffrage was a more immediately realisable aim than any measure of female suffrage. The middle-class leaders of suffrage organisations, conversely, were unable to contemplate working-class men being given the vote before they were.

Emmeline Pankhurst's opponents were rarely polar opposites to her. Often they agreed with her on many issues or even shared her aim of women's suffrage, disagreeing only over means. These internal divisions are at the root of the extraordinary bitterness with which the suffrage story was played out.

Emmeline did not originate the splits in the women's franchise movement but she certainly made her contribution. The Women's Franchise League squandered the enthusiasm of its supporters and what financial resources it had in sectarian infighting. In 1892 Emmeline prepared to disrupt a major meeting at St James's Hall, Piccadilly, in support of the Rollit Bill, brought by the Conservative MP Sir Albert Rollit to give the vote to propertied single women who were eligible to vote in local elections. Emmeline's literature denounced it as *class legislation . . . which, while enfranchising middle-class women and spinsters, denies the vote to the married women of the country and deliberately excludes women lodgers.*[15]

Emmeline and her group arrived early at the hall where the meeting was to take place, leafleted all the seats and were about to take over the platform. When the meeting began, there were heckling and interruptions from the start. An emergency amendment, aimed at undermining the meeting entirely, was sent up from the Pankhursts to the effect that no measure for women's enfranchisement was worth supporting unless it proposed the enfranchisement of all women. This proposition was vigorously debated. A prominent supporter of Emmeline's League, Herbert Burrows, made his way towards the platform despite a threat from the chair that he would be removed. League supporters, seizing their moment, rushed the platform and hand-to-hand fighting followed. The brass railings in front of the stage were torn down and trampled. Emmeline's faction gained control of the platform, from where they led cheers and denounced the bill for attempting to achieve only a part of what they aspired to. It was a foretaste of the divisiveness of Emmeline's tactics.

Putting the case for the vote

The principle that women could vote (though not necessarily stand) in some elections was conceded as early as 1869 when women ratepayers were granted the right to vote in local elections under the Municipal Corporations Act, in an amendment drafted by Richard Pankhurst.

In 1870, school boards were set up all over the country to oversee local education and from the beginning they accepted women both as voters and candidates. Elizabeth Garrett Anderson was the first woman to be elected on to a school board.

In 1888, a Local Government Act was passed and the following year two women were elected to the London County Council. A defeated male candidate, however, successfully protested in the courts that because the new Act had not specifically said women *could* be elected, it must be assumed they could *not* and the women were obliged to resign.

In 1894, under that year's Local Government Act women won the right to serve on parish, urban and rural district councils and property restrictions on candidates to be Poor Law Guardians were abolished (making it easier for women to stand).

In 1907, the Qualification of Women Act made it possible for women to be elected to borough and county councils and to become mayors. Elizabeth Garrett Anderson became the first woman mayor, for Aldeburgh in Suffolk.

Free Speech Agitator

Robert Goulden died suddenly in April 1892. Emmeline did not attend the funeral. There were other shocks for the family to bear. Richard and Emmeline finally decided to stop running the shop into which Emmeline had put so much effort. It had never been a success. Worse still, after they had fulfilled the obligations of a repairing lease on the Russell Square house and paid for extensive building work, they found the house was to be demolished. Their precious fund of money had been wasted.

The Pankhursts needed to live somewhere cheaper and closer to the work Richard still had in Manchester. They decided in early 1893 to leave London, which was a great personal blow to Emmeline who had struggled so to get to the capital. Emmeline was never the most robust of individuals, tending to nervous excitement, stomach complaints and migraines. Her health broke down under the strain of closing the shop and the move, and she went to rest in the seaside resort of Southport near Manchester, where she recovered her strength after a period of depression.

Without the shop to keep up, political meetings to attend or soirees to host, Emmeline spent more time with the children. They had been educated at home in an atmosphere that at least Adela thought of as oppressive. They were 'exhorted to fortitude', Sylvia said later, and expected to bear the miseries of childhood uncomplainingly.[16] Emmeline did not send them to school when they were in London as she said she wanted them to develop their individuality – though when Sylvia was later to demonstrate this quality in disagreements with her mother it was not welcomed. When they moved back to Manchester, to Buckingham Crescent, Victoria Park, the girls went to Manchester High School for Girls.

In many ways Emmeline was a very conventional mother, narrowly middle class in her outlook. When some bigger boys in Russell Square talked to Adela about sex, Emmeline merely criticised the older girls for leaving their young sister alone. Emmeline mumbled haltingly to them that Richard had said she should talk to the girls, without saying what she should talk to the girls about, and the subject of sex was never raised again. Christabel and Sylvia had to remedy their sexual ignorance in what way they could.[17]

Politically Emmeline and Richard moved towards the Independent Labour Party; Emmeline joined and a little later left the Liberals; of whose promises for the enfranchisement of women she had become deeply suspicious. She stood unsuccessfully for the ILP for a position on the Manchester School Board and then was elected to the Chorlton Board of Guardians of the Poor Law in December 1894. The Local Government Act of 1894 had extended to married women the rights to some franchises (female ratepayers had been local electors since 1869) and Emmeline, who rejoiced in a reform for which she had campaigned, was pleased to make use of it. Standing for elections obliged her to make a serious attempt at platform speaking, a talent she was to bring to a high standard over the years.

Keir Hardie (left) joined by a common cause with George Bernard Shaw, 1910

The Independent Labour Party was formed by Keir Hardie and others in 1893 to establish independent socialist candidates in Parliament. It was one of the elements, along with the trade unions and the Fabian Society, that came together in 1900 to form the Labour Representation Committee, which became the Labour party in 1906. The ILP continued to exist within the Labour party, advocating the most radical policies. In December 1923 it had 46 members elected to the House of Commons, contributing to the formation of the first Labour government the following year. It declined in influence after 1946.

Emmeline's organisational abilities immediately came to the fore in improving the lot of inhabitants of the Chorlton Workhouse. She was appalled at the Spartan conditions for the aged poor and the miserably thin cotton frocks worn all year round by little girls of seven and eight as they scrubbed the stones of the long corridors in the institution.

In keeping with advanced thinking in other towns, a country boarding school on the cottage system (children housed in small units where 'house mothers' looked after them) was built for workhouse children so they could be brought up in healthy surroundings and away from their parents and the taint of 'pauperism.' As Sylvia said of her mother: 'Having distressed herself acutely for the unhappy plight of the workhouse children, she now sprang to the opposite extreme, declaring they would be better reared in the new institution than in the average working-class home.'[18]

Emmeline was profoundly affected by her experience of practical work for the poor, particularly illegitimate children. She said *I thought I had been a suffragist before I became a Poor Law Guardian, but now I began to think about the vote in women's hands not only as a right but as a desperate necessity.*[19] The sentiment goes to the heart of what Emmeline Pankhurst thought she was achieving by advancing the cause of women's suffrage: granted the vote, women would have a specific and explicitly superior role to play in social reforms. In believing that women had a special contribution to make on social and educational issues, Emmeline demonstrated how much she was a woman of her time. Even her opponents had long been prepared to allow women to vote in and stand for election to Poor Law and school boards.

Emmeline's hopes for a beneficial female influence seem naïve. While she had a personal, practical contribution to make to improving the lot of the poor, the underlying problem was not whether the workhouse system was in male or female or capable or incapable hands: the system was cruel by nature. It had been subjected to the harshest criticism since it was founded in 1834, not least by Charles Dickens in *Oliver Twist* and George R Simms in *Christmas Day in the Workhouse.*

Richard Pankhurst also joined the Independent Labour Party, in September 1894, thereby further alienating his Liberal client base. Now even clients who had remained loyal to him over his previous disagreements with the Liberal party took their business elsewhere and Manchester City Council stopped using him. He stood as a parliamentary candidate for the ILP for Gorton in July 1895 but, though the Liberal candidate withdrew in his favour, the Conservative still beat him. It was his third and last failure to be elected. Sylvia had *disgraced the family*, Emmeline said, by crying in public at the defeat.[20]

While Pankhurst was in many ways an admirable man, he was probably correct in his long-term assessment of his work and personality before he met Emmeline: that he should not have a family so he would be able to devote himself to his public works. Over and again his principles left his family poorer, worse clothed than they might expect to be, ill-housed and in shabby locations. Though Emmeline never criticised him, he might usefully have added the importance of the security of his own family to his extensive list of principles. The elder girls, Christabel and Sylvia, were deeply engaged in political work and solidly loyal to the family values. Christabel in particular said the family's time in Manchester was the happiest in her recollection. The younger children Adela and Harry, however, found the politics incomprehensible and their father a rather intimidating figure. Harry was a slow learner and Adela lost herself in fantasy and dramas of her own making in which she played all the parts.

The family began to attract major attention because of a particularly asinine decision by Manchester City Corporation that made Emmeline both a martyr and a hero. The ILP habitually held outdoor meetings at an open space called Boggart Hole Clough. After Manchester City Corporation acquired the land, the chair of the parks committee prohibited further ILP meetings. The result of this partisan act of provocation could easily have been predicted: the ILP continued to meet at Boggart Hole, obliging the Corporation to issue a summons against, in the first instance, John Harker, a prominent ILP speaker who had called a meeting. Richard Pankhurst represented him but Harker was found guilty and fined ten shillings (half a pound). Richard appealed against the decision for him.

Emmeline and others repeatedly organised meetings and further prosecutions followed. Emmeline (as yet not prosecuted) then upped the stakes by setting up a collection at a meeting of 4,000, thereby defying another rule, that no money should be collected at public meetings. Emmeline made her first appearance at court in July 1896, along with other ILP members. Sylvia described her: 'She stood there, looking entirely well at ease and self-possessed, wearing an elegant little bonnet of pink straw, her slender, black-gloved hands lying quietly on the rail of the dock before her.'[21] Two men were sent to prison for a month for refusing to pay their fines. Emmeline defiantly declared that not only would she not pay a fine, she would continue to hold meetings and speak at Boggart Hole Clough. The case against her was continually adjourned, the authorities fearing public opinion if they jailed a middle-class lady.

The Corporation's crude attempt to suppress free speech of course attracted vast amounts of attention and far greater crowds than had previously been moved to attend ILP meetings. All Emmeline's diffidence at public speaking disappeared. She spoke to crowds of tens of thousands, stridently defying the Corporation and the courts to do their worst. The ILP celebrated the release of the jailed protesters with processions led by brass bands and ceremonial meals to establish their status as heroes of resistance.

The battle of Boggart Hole Clough was an important lesson in civil disobedience for Emmeline: the authorities had to be goaded to go to the lengths of their power until the disparity between the protesters' action and the authorities' response was so glaring as to tip the balance of sympathy towards the pro-testers. Emmeline was able to gain sympathy for the ILP posi-tion from people who would never support an ILP policy.

Predictably, given the nature of the local government mind, the council then made matters worse by attempting to legitimise the position of the parks committee. The Corporation created a new rule that all meetings in all of its parks were to be banned unless authorised by the parks committee. This only made the situation worse and open to wider civil disobedience. Finally the Home Secretary had to force the council to adopt a by-law granting that no reasonable application for use of the parks for a public meeting would be denied.

It was the high point of their achievement as a couple: Richard had represented the protesters in the courts; Emmeline had played a leading part on the platform. She was elected a member of the National Administrative Council of the ILP on which Richard already sat, the only woman to be so honoured. John Bruce Glasier, a leading ILP member, described her as 'lively as a cricket, full of clever comment, criticism and scandal. I sat quite diverted.'[22]

Richard's health had long been bad: he was suffering from stomach pains that no treatment could alleviate. He was in no better or worse health than usual when, in June 1898, Emmeline took Christabel to Geneva to honour a longstanding arrangement with her old schoolfriend Noémie that if they both had daughters, they would do an 'exchange' so each girl would learn the culture and language of the other. Emmeline hated to leave Richard. She was 'gripped by a sudden fear' as she parted from him, threw her arms around him and begged the 16-year-old Sylvia to *look after father!*[23] She and Christabel travelled at a leisurely pace via Paris to Geneva where they holidayed at Corsier. She regularly corresponded with home. In his last letter her husband of 19 years wrote: 'When you return, we will have a new honeymoon and reconsecrate each to the other in unity of heart. Be Happy.'[24] The next communication Emmeline received was a telegram on 4 July saying that Richard was ill and she should return.

She travelled without pause. On the train from London to Manchester, the last leg of her journey, a man entered her compartment and opened an evening newspaper. She saw in it a black border and the announcement 'Death of Dr Pankhurst'.

Founding the Union: 1898–1905

Richard Pankhurst had died at the age of 58 from a gastric ulcer that had perforated his stomach. He had been reasonably well on the morning of 2 July 1898, given that he was not in good health in general, but took ill that day at lunch and had deteriorated rapidly the following day so Sylvia had called a doctor. By 4 July Sylvia despaired of his life and telegraphed to Emmeline on the Continent but he sank quietly into death that night.

When Emmeline arrived home after midnight on 5 July other family members had already arrived to support Sylvia. The 16-year-old was full of self-reproach for not earlier sending for her mother but Emmeline did not criticise her. Christabel remarked that the sadness that overcame her mother's face at the death of Richard Pankhurst never left her for the rest of her life.

Richard had been hopelessly disorganised; his family realised quite how hopeless after his death. Despite being a lawyer, he had not even left a will. He had left less than £500 but the funeral costs and his debts exceeded that and the family was obliged to sell the furniture and paintings and move to a smaller house in a poorer neighbourhood. The family could have avoided this by a legal procedure that would have shared out Richard's estate among his creditors and written off the debts that remained but Emmeline insisted on the family bearing the burden.

Christabel stayed in Switzerland for the period immediately after her father's death, as Emmeline had asked her to. Emmeline never had great competence in managing a household and their faithful servant Susannah was now married so it fell to the excessively emotional Sylvia to exercise what control she could. Sylvia even took Richard's place in her mother's bed, as Emmeline could not bear to sleep alone.

The family moved to a cheaper property in Nelson Street, another step in their continued progress down the social scale, though it was still a detached house. Emmeline's sister Mary moved back in with the family after her marriage failed, which meant she could take on the burden of running the household. In the proverbial triumph of hope over experience Emmeline opened another fancy goods shop, again called Emersons, which also failed to thrive. Christabel was obliged to put in boring hours working in it; indeed, the shop survived only by the free labour of Emmeline's daughter, sister Mary and brother Walter, who did the book-keeping.

Emmeline had a very middle-class resistance to receiving charity and refused to accept money from an appeal in her husband's name in the *Clarion,* an ILP-supporting socialist newspaper, saying instead that money collected should be used to finance a hall to be used for socialist meetings. She was prepared to accept the proceeds of a more discreet fund collected by wealthy friends of her husband and administered as a trust, though she was to be in almost continuous dispute with the administrators of it. They wanted to retain some of the money for Harry's further education, which they calculated would be expensive, and argued that if the account continued to pay out at the current rate there would be no money left by the time Harry was old enough to need it. This was not a winning argument as far as Emmeline was concerned, who considered the education of girls as important as that of boys. Emmeline felt that by the time Harry was old enough to need support in following a professional career, Emersons would be making sufficient profit to cover the cost. She needed help now.

Harry had suffered a series of childhood illnesses and had poor eyesight, a disability exacerbated by Emmeline's prejudice against spectacles, not allowing him to have a pair. He and Adela were sent, due to their reduced circumstances, to a Board School run by the council, rather than a private school, where Adela was appalled to find she had contracted lice from other children. She was then sent for a while to the Manchester High School for Girls and Harry, who had taken to truancy, was sent away to board at a school in London. Adela was encouraged at school to try for a scholarship to one of the women's colleges at Oxford or Cambridge but Emmeline opposed the idea; the determined Adela continued studying until severe illness meant she had to go to the country to recuperate.

Emmeline herself was not academically gifted. She read novels rather than serious books and skimmed the newspapers. She had resisted Richard's attempts, early in her marriage, to make her follow a course of improving literature. Her notion of self-improvement was to run a shop. Emmeline had encouraged Christabel's passion for ballet and Sylvia's for art – laudable interests for their own sake but unlikely to help the girls become independent at a time when middle-class women were making inroads into the labour market. Both of the elder children had left school at 15, though Christabel would return to education as an adult and Sylvia was subsequently given a free studentship at the Manchester Municipal School of Art after the valuer who came to price the family's pictures for sale saw some of her drawings and realised her talent.

Sylvia was so successful a student as to win a travelling scholarship in 1902, which she used to visit Venice and Florence. Emmeline accompanied her for some of the trip, meeting with her old friend Noémie and shopping in Venice for large quantities of glass to sell in Emersons. She felt herself a benefactor to Manchester for importing these examples of Venetian craftsmanship but they proved unsaleable.

Emmeline had resigned from the Chorlton Board of Guardians as her work there was unpaid and after Richard's death she had to make the most profitable use of her time. The Guardians promptly offered her the paid post of Registrar of Births and Deaths. This gave her an income and an official position in society and fostered her seething sense of injustice as she recorded births to underage mothers who had been impregnated by their own fathers or some male relative. Emmeline remarked: *there was nothing that could be done in most cases. The age of consent in England is sixteen years, but a man can always claim he thought the girl was over sixteen.*[25] The law at this time permitted a defence that the man had 'reasonable cause to believe' the girl was over 16, though this could hardly have been the case with family members. In future years Emmeline was repeatedly to cite social reform as the primary practical reason for women's suffrage, though the laws on the age of consent and incest were promulgated in 1885 and 1908 respectively, when women had no parliamentary rights, and Parliament found no need to make extensive improvements to them after women received the vote. With her finances more stable, Emmeline was able to return to political work and she accepted the ILP nomination for the Manchester School Board, on which she sat from November 1900. School boards were abolished by the 1902 Education Act and replaced by new local education authorities, to which women, to their disgust, were not eligible for election. The government quickly realised this was a retrograde step, as women had been able to be elected to school boards for 30 years, and obliged local education authorities to co-opt women members. Emmeline was promptly co-opted and remained a member until 1904.

Year	Total population	Electorate	As percentage of adult population[26]
1900	41,155,000	6,730,935	27
1910	44,915,000	7,694,741	28
1919	44,599,000	21,755,583	78
1929	46,679,000	28,850,870	90

Christabel was increasingly taking an active interest in women's suffrage under the influence of new young women friends she had met while attending open classes at Owens College. She then went on to take a law degree, and so ended the aimlessness of her late teens and early 20s. Emmeline and she were perturbed to find that the ILP had marginalised the issue of women's suffrage. Some of its members regarded women's suffrage as a middle-class distraction from Labour politics; conventional socialist thinking

Christabel Pankhurst, destined to be the first militant

said the divisions in society were based on class, not gender. This was true only to a limited extent: a middle-class woman may have had more freedom, comfort and opportunity than a working-class man, but women were suffering disabilities within their class that were gender-based.

While Sylvia was painting murals in the hall which had been built in St James Road in Salford to commemorate her father, she discovered something which starkly revealed the real priorities of the ILP: the hall, due to be opened on 3 October 1903, was to be used by an ILP branch which did not admit women. The Pankhursts were outraged that Pankhurst Hall, decorated at no charge by Sylvia and dedicated to Richard's work, was to be the scene of an injustice against which Richard Pankhurst had always fought. At the opening ceremony addressed by socialist artist Walter Crane, Emmeline refused to speak to the leading ILP members Philip Snowden and John Bruce Glasier.

We must have an independent women's movement, she told women friends. *Come to my house tomorrow and we will arrange it.*[27] Thus on 10 October 1903 a group of women socialists met at the Nelson Street house and voted to approve what became the Women's Social and Political Union. Unlike the Women's Franchise League, it was to be a single-sex membership organisation.

The absurd injustice that drove Emmeline to form the WSPU was so egregious it has tended to obscure the ambiguities of Emmeline's decision. Confronted with a single-sex club, Emmeline formed a single-sex pressure group. Whatever moral arguments she had against a gender ban operated by others were therefore qualified by her own gender ban. It was, moreover, though a female membership organisation, one in which the work of men played an essential part. Hardie and East End MP George Lansbury, for example, who were totally committed to the principle of women's suffrage, were needed to do the technical work of bringing forward and arguing parliamentary bills.

The First Militancy

Deeds not words was to be our permanent motto, declared Emmeline about the founding of the Women's Social and Political Union, though the first two years of the organisation, to 1905, found it involved in the same kind of activity as other suffrage societies: building membership and sending out visiting speakers to ILP and trade union functions and other gatherings that were likely to support them.[28] At this stage the WSPU operated as a ginger group, applying pressure to the political left to ensure it was fully behind women's suffrage. They were officially free from party affiliation, but so many of them were members of the ILP that they were sometimes wrongly considered to be the women's section of the socialist party.

One new recruit was Teresa Billington, a schoolteacher who had approached Emmeline in her capacity as a member of the Manchester School Board as Billington, an agnostic, wished to be relieved of the obligation of teaching religious education. Emmeline could not help and Billington eventually went to teach in a Jewish school where gentiles were not expected to teach religion. However, the link was made. Billington found Emmeline 'as gracious,

VOTES FOR WOMEN.

MRS. T. BILLINGTON-GREIG
HON. ORGANISING SEC. WOMEN'S FREEDOM LEAGUE
1, ROBERT STREET, ADELPHI, LONDON, W.C.

Teresa Billington, known as 'the woman with the whip', which she used to protect herself during militant demonstrations

dominant and lovely as she was always to be' but formed an impression of her rigidity as well: 'You might have offered some variation of agreement, some indication of a differing view. But this was ignored. You left her feeling that without any definite committal on her part or agreement on yours, the line of action to be taken was settled.'[29]

Billington was drawn into the WSPU, becoming one of the Union's first five speakers, along with Emmeline and her three daughters. All were members of the ILP and Emmeline worked with the ILP until 1905, being re-elected to its National Administrative Council in spring of that year. She found it easy to obtain full approval for policies calling for women's suffrage on the same basis as men, but as the same delegates also supported complete adult suffrage, this did not resolve the suffrage movement's conflicting interests. She was still asking the working class to support a measure which, by giving women the vote on the same basis by which men currently held it – that is, to those who owned property – would increase the number of Conservative and Liberal voters at a time when the tiny ILP needed all the votes it could get.

John Bruce Glasier, chairman of the ILP and formerly a good friend, viewed Emmeline and her group with deep suspicion, remarking on the vanity and idleness of Christabel and his feeling that the Pankhursts were middle-class opportunists taking what they could from the Labour movement while not respecting its principles, not 'seeking democratic freedom but self-importance'. He recorded how he berated Emmeline, one night at Nelson Street, scorning 'their miserable individualist sexism'.[30]

Emmeline's experiences as a widow seem to have made her view of men more negative than it had been previously. She declared herself completely against what she assumed in 1905 would be a Liberal proposal to give all men a vote. Sylvia reported her saying: *Unless women got inside the constitution before the introduction of manhood suffrage, they would never get in at all; never . . . they would be afraid of womanhood suffrage, because it would place women in a majority.*[31]

Women's suffrage was a tired force when the WSPU was founded; the National Union of Women's Suffrage Societies had given up hope of a government bill but held an annual lobby of

Sylvia Pankhurst was an accomplished artist and designer whose work gave the WSPU a coherent visual identity.

Parliament to call for private members' bills and to hear friendly MPs express friendly sentiments. Emmeline attended in 1904 but gave an early taste of what was to come when she insulted a leading MP by insisting he tell them what he was going to do for women's suffrage, alienating both MPs and women from suffrage organisations with her manner.

Sylvia was living in London while she took up a scholarship at the Royal College of Art. Emmeline stayed with her in February 1905 while they worked with Keir Hardie, now MP for Merthyr Tydfil, to find an MP who had drawn a high position in the ballot for private members' bills and persuade him to bring in a Women's Enfranchisement Bill. This was the first women's bill for eight years and that it was even set down was entirely due to the lobbying efforts of Emmeline and Keir Hardie's dedication and parliamentary skills.

James Keir Hardie

James Keir Hardie (1856-1915) was the illegitimate son of Mary Keir, a servant from Lanarkshire, Scotland. He was sent to work as a baker's delivery boy aged eight without any education, and, though his mother had married David Hardie, the boy was at one time the sole wage earner of the family. At the age of 11, he became a coal miner. By 17 he had taught himself to read and write and began to take an interest in trade unions. He formed a union at his colliery and led the first ever strike of Lanarkshire miners in 1881. He began to rise through the ranks of Scottish unionists and stood unsuccessfully as Independent Labour candidate for Mid-Lanark.

In 1892 he stood as Independent Labour candidate for West Ham South in East London and became the first Labour MP. In 1893 he called for the formation of the Independent Labour Party. At its opening conference he was elected chairman and leader. He lost his London seat in 1895 but was elected as MP for Merthyr Tydfil in 1900 as one of only two Labour MPs. He organised a pact with the Liberals that the two parties should not stand against each other in a number of constituencies. As a result, Labour had 29 MPs in 1906 and 40 in 1910 when George Barnes replaced Hardie as leader of the party.

Hardie's pacifism inspired him, even while fatally ill, to attempt to organise a national strike in opposition to the First World War. He was a visionary supporter of high income tax for high earners, old-age pensions, women's suffrage, the payment of MPs, the abolition of the House of Lords, self-rule in India and equal rights for non-whites in South Africa.

In terms of Emmeline's biography, the question of when Hardie and Sylvia became lovers is less important than that of when Emmeline found out about it. Certainly Hardie had given much-needed support when Sylvia was alone in London and he and her brother Harry (at school in London) were her only friends. Later, when she moved into new rooms in Chelsea she described how 'I sat among my boxes, ill and lonely, when all unexpected Keir Hardie came knocking at my door. He took command . . . he lifted heavy things into position and when all was in order, took me out for a meal at a little Italian restaurant.'[32]

Hardie showed a dedication to 'the woman question' and, most importantly, to Emmeline's approach to suffrage based on gender rather than class, that suggests a deeper motivation than the cause alone, particularly as he had to countermand explicit instructions from his party in order to forward motions for the Pankhursts.

Sylvia was 22 years old in 1904; Hardie was 26 years older than her, three years more than the age difference between her mother and her father. If the age difference was an issue to others, it need not have been to them. Hardie was a man of dynamic action: 'to me, he was a tremendous hero' Sylvia wrote.[33] Sylvia was a passionate and lonely young woman. She needed a lover and an older man to replace her father; Keir Hardie offered both capacities in one person and his wife was so far away – in Scotland – that perhaps sex with him did not feel like adultery. The great danger of sexual relations at the time, pregnancy, was probably not a major concern as they moved in circles in which information about contraception had been a major political cause and they would have knowledge of and access to contraception. Whether in 1904 or a couple of years later, they became sexual partners, which introduced a charge into the relationship between mother, daughters and their principal parliamentary supporter. Hardie's colleagues knew he was entranced by the Pankhursts but believed, as Glasier wrote, that Emmeline was 'the Delilah who had cut our Sampson's locks'.[34]

Regardless of the jibes, Emmeline and Hardie had achieved more in a few weeks of lobbying than the national suffrage societies had in years of polite requests. The older suffrage societies organised in support of the bill, none the less, holding a tame meeting with well-mannered women applauding MPs who pledged their support. At the reading of the Women's Enfranchisement Bill on 12 May 1905 Emmeline was one of some 300 women in the lobby of the House of Commons. The bill was a Second Order of the day, following a First Order measure to compel carts to carry a rear light at night. Hardie had pleaded with its sponsors to withdraw it, without success. The opponents of women's suffrage were able to extend the debate on this bill with parliamentary jocularities until four o'clock.

The Liberal MP Bamford Slack then rose to move the second reading of the Women's Enfranchisement Bill – the beginning of its journey through the parliamentary system towards becoming law. Henry Labouchere rose to oppose it. Labouchere was a noted rake, wit and radical – he was against the House of Lords and the established Church – with some extraordinarily un-radical views. He had, for example, proposed the amendment to the Sexual Law Amendment Bill of 1885 which had made all homosexual acts illegal whether in public or private. Now he opposed women's suffrage in the usual terms: '. . . if women came into political life they must accept the conditions equally with men. The polite deference to women in drawing rooms did not obtain in politics . . . To give the franchise to women would destroy the best relation between the sexes. Think of a married man after having heard speeches maundering on all the evening having to go over the whole again with his wife and daughters. They might be on opposite sides, and it would mean the destruction of the social relations that had existed from time immemorial.'[35]

The bill was thus talked out – it ran out of parliamentary time – to Emmeline's unconcealed disgust. Many of the moderate National Union of Women's Suffrage Society members withdrew but Emmeline rallied the remaining women in the lobby to follow her outside for a protest meeting against the government. The elderly Elizabeth Wolstenholme Elmy began to speak to the crowd but the police jostled them and ordered them to disperse. Emmeline imperiously demanded of the police where they could meet. Doubtless nonplussed and unused to such requests, a police inspector let them proceed to Broad Sanctuary, near the gates of Westminster Abbey, though under the

Metropolitan Police Act of 1839 demonstrations were forbidden in the vicinity of the Houses of Parliament while a sitting was taking place.

This was the first militant act of the WSPU according to Emmeline: a militancy that challenged expectations of ladylike middle-class behaviour.[36] Other women's leaders had created formidable protest movements, Josephine Butler's opposition to the Contagious Diseases Acts being the best example, but they had used a Victorian conception of women and femininity. Emmeline and her followers were resisting a passive role and taking the initiative.

Despite Emmeline's indignation at the tone of Labouchere's remarks, Labouchere was correct in saying women's suffrage would alter the domestic balance. If women's suffrage did not precipitate such changes, why fight for it? Emmeline could not be both a militant street fighter and a little woman in the house. Her later complaints about the coarseness of the debate used the same concepts of womanhood as Labouchere, but her actions were already pointing her in quite another direction.

Emmeline fully realised that she was doing something new but she was still feeling out the precise strategy. One thing she was sure of was that she did not want to pursue the path of the NUWSS with their polite, middle-class meetings that got nowhere. True to its origins among ILP activists, the WSPU took to addressing working-class audiences at open-air fairs

Annie Kenney was the only working-class woman to become part of the senior hierarchy of the WSPU.

where their new recruit, former factory girl Annie Kenney, spoke to her own in their own language. Annie, whose mother had died in 1905, had been taken in by Emmeline and had become like another, intensely loyal, daughter to her.

The next strategic goal was targeting not backbench MPs but those who would form part of a new government after the imminent general election. Emmeline had moved past the stage of asking; she wanted to demand the vote. To this end, Emmeline and some trusted supporters, including Christabel, Annie Kenney and Teresa Billington, discussed making the leap into direct action. On 13 October 1905 Christabel left the house with Annie, saying to Emmeline: 'We will get our question answered or sleep in prison tonight.'[37]

The two women attended a meeting at the Free Trade Hall in Manchester where the future Foreign Secretary Sir Edward Grey was speaking. After he had spoken Kenney stood up and shouted out: 'Will the Liberal government give women the vote?' There was no answer and Christabel unfolded a fabric 'Votes for Women' banner she had hidden in her blouse and shouted the question again; to the fury of the meeting. To maintain the peace, the chief constable of Manchester approached the demonstrators and invited them to put their question in writing so it could be handed to the speaker, which they did. Sir Edward then responded to the vote of thanks but did not answer the question. Kenney stood on her chair and shouted the question again, as did Christabel, so stewards roughly manhandled the two shouting women to an anteroom where police asked them to behave themselves and said they could leave.

Instead Christabel spat, or attempted to spit, in the faces of two policemen in order to commit a 'technical assault' and struck one of them, an Inspector Mather, in the mouth. The police took them downstairs to the street and asked them to leave. Christabel struck Mather again and both women started shouting and attracting public attention until the police arrested them.

The following morning Annie and Christabel were charged with disorderly behaviour, causing an obstruction and assaulting the police. Christabel admitted the offences but said they were obliged to commit acts of civil disobedience as a result of the legal position of women: 'We cannot make an orderly protest because we have not the means whereby citizens may do such a thing.'[38] The magistrates imposed small fines with an alternative of seven days in jail for Christabel and three for Annie. Emmeline pleaded with them to let her pay the fines so they could go home, having made their point. Christabel insisted: 'Mother, if you pay my fine I will never go home.'[39] They were both driven off to prison, the WSPU's first martyrs.

Direct Action: 1905–1907

Martyrdom had two facets for the WSPU: the act itself, and the publicity it generated. Teresa Billington had been going to join the protesters but eventually stayed back and worked on drumming up press interest. This was a spectacular success; the events in Manchester were widely reported, even by papers that had no interest in women's suffrage. As Christabel wrote triumphantly: 'The long, long newspaper silence as to woman suffrage was broken.'[40]

The principal aim of the protest had been achieved: women's suffrage had risen up the agenda. The suffragists even had a new slogan. Their banner had been going to call for 'Women's Suffrage' but at the last minute they had changed it. 'Votes for Women' was a slogan for the 20th century: direct and to the point.

Even at this first stage, however, some suffragists were complaining that the Pankhursts had not furthered the cause of women's suffrage but damaged it. Standing on chairs, shouting and spitting, so the argument went, were not the kind of behaviour that would earn women respect for their judgement and show they were fit to vote.

There was more in this criticism than fastidiousness. Even Christabel was embarrassed at the nature of the 'assault' she had committed by spitting at the policemen, to the extent that she began to speak about it evasively at meetings, almost to the point of denying she had ever done it. Had she spat at the policemen or not? She probably had tried to but in the dry-mouthed excitement of the moment was not able to do so. Striking Inspector Mather (though physical violence was not part of the plan) was probably the best symbolic assault she could manage in the circumstances.

Spitting did not become one of the weapons in the Pankhurst armoury of protest. The uncertainty as to what Christabel should admit to having done indicates the difficulty women found in creating a militant role for themselves. Christabel had, it was alleged in court, complained that women should not be man-handled in the way she was in the Free Trade Hall, but it was difficult to square this with her provocative behaviour and the fact that she was demanding rights previously accorded only to some men.

Emmeline, fearful before Christabel and Annie went off that night and eager to pay their fines, did not immediately grasp the potential of the militant strategy but she very quickly came to understand how the lessons of the battle of Boggart Hole Clough and the organising abilities learned from the trade union move-ment could be harnessed in the WSPU to further the cause of women's suffrage. Emmeline's genius as a leader was never her far-sightedness, but her ability time and again to seize the moment and rally her forces to act decisively before her oppo-nents had time to know what was happening.

The night of the sentencing, while Christabel and Annie were in prison, Emmeline called a meeting in Stevenson Square to protest at the punishment. Nearly 1,000 people attended. A crowd of 2,000 met Annie on her release on 16 October and on the day of Christabel's release, 20 October, there was a huge rally at the Free Trade Hall at which the two women spoke and received bouquets and Keir Hardie condemned the treatment the women had received.

Emmeline and Christabel's burgeoning militancy put their livelihoods at risk: the family's only income was Emmeline's salary from her job as a Registrar (the shop was as ever making no money) and as a public official she ought not to be politically controversial. Christabel was attending Owens College, studying for a law degree, and was required, under threat of expulsion, to sign a pledge not to participate in further disturbances. She may have agreed to do so out of self-interest, but she may also have calculated that a trained lawyer would be rather more use to the WSPU than an expelled student. She had, moreover, already done her bit: women's suffrage was now clearly on the agenda for the general election, called for January 1906, and new recruits were pouring into the dynamic organisation.

Emmeline made maximum use of the excitement generated by the election and the WSPU's protests. She travelled widely to address ILP meetings on 'Women and Socialism' and called on other WSPU members to attend meetings conducted by the members of the Liberal cabinet that was serving as a caretaker government following the resignation of the Conservative Prime Minister A J Balfour in December 1905. This strategy was not an unequivocal success: the barracking definitely put off some prospective MPs. Winston Churchill (a prime target, being the only member of the caretaker government standing in a Manchester constituency) had supported women's suffrage but now declared himself opposed, if militants were going to 'hen-peck' him. The election resulted in a Liberal landslide with a respectable number of Labour MPs elected (29 including Keir Hardie) and the WSPU established as a real political force. They even had a distinguishing name now, an insulting diminutive applied to them by the *Daily Mail* but which they embraced: the suffragettes.

Christabel was keen for the movement to operate from London, as a parliamentary pressure group ought to be near Parliament but, though Emmeline still yearned to live in London, the years of privation had taught her some money sense. She insisted they could not afford it, and instead they sent as an emissary Annie Kenney, who would live with supporters and 'rouse London'. Kenney first set out to contact poor women in the East End, another step in the radicalisation of the WSPU, which had now moved beyond the middle-class base of the suffrage movement and was organising the working class.

Kenney and her London supporters planned a women's rally on the day of the opening of the new parliament, 19 February 1906. When Emmeline arrived in London she was appalled to find they had booked the enormous Caxton Hall, near to Parliament; she thought the meeting would be an embarrassment, just a handful of supporters rattling around in a huge room. Sylvia and Hardie called on East End MP George Lansbury, who with his daughters was a keen supporter of women's suffrage, and they rounded up East End support. On the day the hall was full to its 700 capacity with more women outside. Annie Kenney was speaking when the news came through that the King's Speech did not mention women's suffrage. As Annie took her seat Emmeline, as usual in command of the situation in an instant, moved a resolution that the meeting should at once proceed to the House of Commons to

Frederick Pethick Lawrence

Emmeline Pethick Lawrence

lobby members. It was raining and bitterly cold but the gathering took up this adventure. 'They followed her to a woman,' wrote Sylvia, 'though many of them had never set eyes on her before.'[41] They waited in the cold and wet outside the House of Commons while relays of 20 were allowed in to lobby MPs. *They were prepared to do something that women had never done before – fight for themselves,* Emmeline said, *for their own human rights. Our militant movement was established.*[42] The press attention further publicised Emmeline's position and emphasised that the WSPU was now the primary force in the women's suffrage cause.

The WSPU was still a pressure group with more enthusiasm than organisation. In 1906 Hardie introduced Emmeline to Emmeline Pethick Lawrence, a wealthy activist whose husband Frederick was also a radical. Emmeline Pankhurst was unsuccessful in her attempts to woo her but Annie Kenney won her heart. The London WSPU committee now became the national committee. Pethick Lawrence put the movement on a sound financial footing and her husband became business manager. The campaigners first operated from a spare room in the Pethick Lawrences' London flat in Clement's Inn but in September 1906 they took over the lower floor of Clement's Inn, which had become vacant, as WSPU headquarters. The following year they set up the newspaper *Votes for Women*; each new subscriber received a free picture of Emmeline.

There was a blow from the Labour MPs: after so many years of waiting without power, the new MPs, now in an electoral coalition with the Liberals, had their own programme. The right to put private members' bills was allocated by drawing lots in what was called the parliamentary ballot. Though Keir Hardie was their leader, they did not allow him to dictate which bills should be put forward, instead deciding to allocate the places they drew in the ballot to those causes that had the most supporters. Their measures were valuable and responsible, to do with school meals, old-age pensions and the right to work, but Emmeline, with the campaigner's faith that one reform would change everything, argued that *when women had won the vote, such matters would be dealt with as a matter of course*.[43] She pleaded with Hardie to influence his colleagues. He did his best and promised that if he himself drew a ballot place for a resolution he would devote it to the cause without consulting his colleagues. It was not enough for Emmeline. She seemed not to realise the personal sacrifice Hardie was making when he had so few friends: he had retained his role as leader of the parliamentary party by just one vote.

That April Hardie did put down a resolution (a statement of principle, rather than a bill which could be enacted in law) 'that sex should cease to be a bar to the exercise of the parliamentary franchise'. He was waiting to speak on it when Emmeline and her followers, sitting in the ladies' gallery and fearing the resolution would be 'talked out' (thereby misunderstanding the parliamentary procedure – as it was a resolution, not a bill, it had a good chance of being voted on) started shouting and throwing flags down into the chamber saying 'Votes for Women'. The MPs were angered by the WSPU's lack of respect for Parliament; worse still, Hardie had been embarrassed in front of his parliamentary colleagues, with whom he already had enough difficulties. His resolution fell without a vote and he left without speaking to Emmeline.

Direct action was to Emmeline clearly a better way. A deputation went to 10 Downing Street to lobby Campbell-Bannerman, the Prime Minister. When he did not see them, they sat on the steps and refused to move. A week later another deputation tried the same tactics, though this time Annie Kenney jumped on the Prime Minister's motor car and began to deliver a speech. She and two others were arrested but the Prime Minister asked the police to release them in order to deny them the publicity of a court appearance. He also agreed to see a suffragette deputation.

Emmeline had a WSPU contingent march from the statue of Boadicea on Westminster Bridge to where the meeting was to be held at the Foreign Office and then on to Trafalgar Square. The Prime Minister saw some 306 delegates representing suffragists, Emmeline's suffragettes, trades councils and temperance societies. It is a testament to the eminence Emmeline's organisation had achieved in only three years that she was one of the seven women speakers. The Prime Minister's response started well: 'You have made out before the country a conclusive and irrefutable case', he said, but he went on to tell the meeting that he had a long legislative programme and his cabinet was not united on the issue of women's suffrage so a bill in the near future was unlikely.[44]

All this convinced Emmeline that women's suffrage would never find its own place on the parliamentary agenda. Continued militancy was its only hope. She sanctioned a campaign of harassment of ministers both on the platform and in their homes over the next two years. The WSPU, adopting the strategy used in the Irish parliamentary disruptions of the late 19th century, focused their efforts solely on members of the government – regardless of their opinions – while ignoring other parties. Liberal supporters of women's suffrage such as Lloyd George were targets while leading anti-suffrage parliamentarians on the Tory side were not.

Anticipating trouble, stewards in political meetings took to ejecting suffragettes even if they were asking questions at the time appointed to do so. This heavy-handed approach proved counter-productive as it stimulated outrage and support for the suffragettes. The president of the Women's Liberal Association in Northampton resigned her office and joined the WSPU after seeing Emmeline thrown out of a hall for asking a question of Herbert Asquith.

Through 1906 the WSPU disrupted Liberal party meetings, held demonstrations and suffered imprisonment. The experience of protest was exciting and novel for many women though sometimes unpleasant too, such as when thugs broke up their open-air meetings by throwing mice, flour and tomatoes.

Prison terms for protest activity were now common and militants courted imprisonment by deliberately provocative actions such as slapping the hands of policemen who were attempting to restrain them. Thus Adela, now an elementary school teacher, earned her week in Strangeways and, when she re-emerged, a fulsome welcome from her mother and a supportive crowd.

The political activity put a strain on the family's finances and Emmeline again had to move to a cheaper home, on Upper Brook Street in Manchester, where she continued her work as a Registrar. Emmeline's sister Mary often did Emmeline's work for her when she was away for political activities. Emersons was finally closed in belated recognition that the Pankhursts were not successful shopkeepers. Christabel passed her law degree at Owens College and took up the post of chief organiser for the WSPU at a salary of two pounds ten shillings a week. She moved to London and lived with the Pethick Lawrences in their comfortable home in Clement's Inn.

Now the WSPU was enjoying some popular success, paid posts also went to Adela and Annie Kenney. Sylvia, who had previously hosted WSPU visitors, found the movement increasingly filling up her life and her tiny apartment. She wanted to devote herself to art. She resigned as honorary secretary of the WSPU and wrote to her mother explaining that she wanted to apply for a free studentship to complete her course. Emmeline did not bother to reply. Sylvia had been a most dutiful daughter, writing to her mother every second day when they were apart. Now, she explained, 'my last letter unanswered, I ceased to write at all, except on matters of importance.'[45] Emmeline's family was splitting under the strain.

Tearing up the Constitution

The family was split, in part, by the women's different political stands. The WSPU had been born close to the ILP and Sylvia, particularly under the influence of Keir Hardie, had remained a dedicated socialist, seeing the disability of women as one among many inequities of society. Christabel was no natural socialist and had made it WSPU policy to oppose all parliamentary candidates, using by-elections not as a platform for supporting a pro-women's suffrage candidate, but for demonstrating the power of the WSPU to disrupt the political process. This seemed mischievously destructive at the time but it helped the WSPU to break away from the Labour movement and it addressed an underlying problem: by 1906 a majority in the House of Commons had supported the principle of women's suffrage for at least 20 years. Because that support was spread across all parties, however, a suffrage campaign based on a particular party would be doomed to failure as it could not count on the support of suffrage advocates in other parties. Women's suffrage had to be forced onto the national agenda.

Emmeline remained a socialist but, as she was always to do now, deferred to her elder daughter's judgement. Her journey away from Labour accelerated after, early in 1907, she watched the Labour party conference reject a motion for women's suffrage brought by Hardie. By almost three to one the delegates voted instead for adult suffrage – votes for all men and women. Later that year Emmeline and Christabel resigned from the ILP.

At a demonstration in the lobby of the House of Commons in October 1906, Emmeline was thrown to the floor in a confused rush and 11 women were arrested including Adela, Annie Kenney, Teresa Billington and Emmeline Pethick Lawrence. They were sentenced to be bound over to keep the peace or to two months' imprisonment. All chose the latter and Sylvia went to prison too, for protesting their imprisonment at the court. Frederick Pethick Lawrence later went to visit his wife in Holloway and found her 'heading for a nervous breakdown' from shock at the unaccustomed conditions. He told Emmeline Pankhurst he was going to free her, and Emmeline at first made a scornful remark about the attitude of husbands but he begged and she eventually acquiesced. Frederick later remarked with pride how his wife later 'won a victory over herself by conquering fear'.[46]

There was still enough excitement at suffragettes' imprisonment for thorough press coverage of the trial and the gathering at Caxton Hall afterwards where Emmeline presided over a fundraising meeting. The widespread sympathy for the prisoners, and Keir Hardie's intervention, led the Home Secretary to allow the women to be in the 'first division' of incarceration, meaning that they could wear their own clothes and have access to writing materials. Emmeline and Christabel's tactics were winning the propaganda battle. They had tapped into a reservoir of need among middle-class women not just for democratic representation but also for excitement and a release from the dull drawing-room existence of an Edwardian lady. Increasingly WSPU supporters were fashionable ladies in silks and satins, meeting in Emmeline Pethick Lawrence's rooms in Clement's Inn. It was no place for downtrodden working-class women. Working-class supporters would not have been deliberately excluded, but the space chosen for the meetings was not their natural habitat.

The way forward for the WSPU was now obvious: to raise the stakes by moving from a small number of arrests incidental to the main activity, to demonstrations to encourage mass arrest. The WSPU openly appealed for 'prison volunteers' to attend a women's parliament at Caxton Hall on 13 February 1907, to protest at the failure, again, of the government to introduce a women's suffrage measure in the King's Speech. Again, Emmeline roused the meeting to march to the Houses of

Parliament, supposedly to lobby the Prime Minister. Veteran campaigner Charlotte Despard led about 400 women forth. They met rows of police, including mounted police, who rode into the procession to break it up. Even as they were being dispersed, more and more contingents of women tried to get through. The battle lasted five hours and left many women with bruises and torn clothes.

Fifty-nine appeared in court, including Christabel, Sylvia and the elderly Charlotte Despard, and were sentenced to between one and three weeks. Outside their supporters praised the heroism of the women in rousing speeches: *If the government brings out the horse guards and fires on us we will not flinch* said Emmeline.[47] Another rush at the Commons a month later resulted in 74 arrests.

Emmeline did not herself seek imprisonment for fear of losing her Registrar's position, already under threat after an anonymous complaint to her employer. She eventually felt obliged to resign the post, a genuine sacrifice as it was not only remunerative work but carried with it a pension. In its stead the Union paid her from £200 to £300 a year for her duties as a speaker; her sister Mary also drew a salary from the Union. The money generated by fund-raising around the mass imprisonments meant that the WSPU employed 32 people by 1908 and had an income of more than £20,000 in 1908–9. One of their wealthy supporters gave money for a motor car so that Emmeline could travel more comfortably.

With success came dissent. When the Pankhurst family was keeping the militant suffrage movement alive through personal sacrifice, no one complained of their dominance. As the movement grew so spectacularly, those who had helped it to do so – more practical women such as Emmeline Pethick Lawrence, Teresa Billington and Charlotte Despard – also wanted a share in its direction.

Emmeline faced her first revolt at the annual conference sched-
uled for 12 October 1907, where several leading members were
planning to put the WSPU on a more democratic footing.
Emmeline had no skill at manipulating the machinery of democracy, but was adept at conspiracy. She needed powerful friends
and so first made sure Emmeline Pethick Lawrence was on her
side. Mrs Pethick Lawrence confirmed her personal loyalty to
Emmeline and Christabel; she did not want to see the organisation's leadership weakened (as she saw it) by being vested in a
committee. Emmeline Pethick Lawrence later declared: 'I shall
never forget the gesture with which she swept from the board all
the "pros and cons" which had caused us sleepless nights. *I shall
tear up the constitution* she declared.'[48]

Emmeline was now in a position to strike first. She cancelled
the October conference and called an 'urgent' meeting for 10
September. The afternoon of the meeting the old committee was
gathered together to hear Emmeline annul the constitution of
the WSPU and list the new committee members, excluding the
rebels Billington and Despard. That evening the meeting took
place at the Exeter Hall and Emmeline read out the list of the
new committee. Only Londoners were invited, so it was hardly
representative of a national organisation, but Emmeline was not
prepared to put the decision to a vote, even at this stage. An
organisation campaigning for democracy for women had denied
democracy to its own members. Teresa Billington (now married
and called Billington-Greig) called Emmeline a 'dictator' and
remarked, it seems half-admiringly, on her 'quick instinct for
effect and that political unscrupulousness that mark her out'.[49]

Yet, as Frederick Pethick Lawrence noted, 'Mrs Pankhurst,
though theoretically the autocrat of the WSPU, did not, in fact,
during the years that immediately followed, choose to exercise
any direct personal control. A consummate evangelist, she preferred to expound the gospel of militancy in an endless succes-

Emmeline Pankhurst arrested outside Parliament. This lead to her first imprisonment for six weeks, 13 February 1908

sion of great meetings up and down the country.' The control of the day-to-day business of the Union passed to a 'triumvirate' of Christabel, Emmeline Pethick Lawrence and her husband Frederick.[50]

The breakaway suffragettes formed a rebel organisation, eventually called the Women's Freedom League, which at its height had 61 branches to the WSPU's 90 – though the WSPU was less interested in forming branches than in having individual agitators working in districts. The split resulted in the loss of many working-class members from the WSPU as many of the northern branches went over to the rebels and the almost complete loss of Scotland and Wales, which each had just three WSPU branches remaining. With characteristic honesty Billington-Greig was to concede that in a very short time the Freedom League 'dropped steadily to a position of mediocrity', though it continued as an undistinguished political organisation.[51]

The infighting contributed to Sylvia's isolation. Emmeline ignored her younger daughter's gentle reassurance: 'Do not fear the democratic constitution. You can carry the conference with you.'[52] Sylvia was probably right: Emmeline almost certainly could have won the day had she put her personal authority behind an appeal to the democratically representative conference that she had cancelled.

As a test for every member following the split, each had to sign a pledge saying they would not endorse candidates of any political party until women had the vote. That would put paid to the strong Labour and lingering Liberal influences in the WSPU and ensure that members' overriding loyalty would be to the Pankhursts and the WSPU. In her defence, Emmeline said her suffragettes were *purely a volunteer army, and no one is obliged to remain in it*; they must obey orders or leave.[53] The coming years would show quite how far she would make this army go.

Imprisonment: 1908–1910

The suffragette army forged in the wake of the 1907 split, with its brass bands, processions, open-air meetings, uniforms, and single dominant family, had more than a little in common with the Salvation Army. The emotional and symbolic echoes of revivalist religion were even more obvious. The suffragettes were absolutely convinced of their rectitude and believed that ultimate redemption (when the franchise was won) would usher in a paradisal time of social progress. The 'martyrdom' of prison and 'suffering for the cause' were suffused with religious imagery, as were such events as the self-denial week, in which activists took on the abstinence normally associated with Lent and refrained from using butter, sugar, meat and sweets so the money saved could be offered up to the movement.

Women's Sunday in Hyde Park, London, 21 June 1908, the largest demonstration ever held

The seven processions marching to Hyde Park on 21 June 1908 at the Union's largest ever demonstration emphasised the martial spirit of the organisation. All the women marched in white with trimmings of green and purple, following Emmeline Pethick Lawrence's colour scheme of white for purity, green for hope and purple for dignity. Processions replete with regalia marched to bands playing the music to stirring suffrage songs. A chief marshal directed the march with group marshals, banner marshals, group captains, stewards and sergeants under her command. Perhaps half a million people eventually attended Women's Day in Hyde Park, the largest demonstration in the history of the country to that date. There were 20 platforms from which speakers addressed the nearest crowds. Banners picturing Emmeline the great leader fluttered among the hundreds being borne aloft in the bright sunshine. In its charismatic, autocratic leadership and understanding of spectacle the WSPU now looked forward to the European political movements of the 1920s and 30s, though without their vicious streak.

The Union's principles were now clearly enunciated in a way which would not alienate the middle class by supporting votes for the working class: 'Object: To secure for women the Parliamentary Vote as it is or may be granted to men . . . The Women's Social and Political Union are NOT asking for a vote for every woman, but simply that sex shall cease to be a disqualification for the franchise.'[54]

WSPU MERCHANDISE

Address Books	two shillings
Bags (in leather)	ten shillings and sixpence each
Blotters	one shilling
Crêpe de Chine motor scarves	six shillings and 11 pence
Handkerchiefs (bordered in the colours)	six shillings and 11 pence
Hat pins (in the colours)	sixpence

Stationery, fancy boxes	one shilling
Postcard albums	three shillings and sixpence
'Votes for Women' buttons	a penny

Votes for Women 13 August 1909
At prices like these, most suffragette merchandise would have been beyond working-class pockets. A housemaid at this time would earn between four and sixpence and eight and sixpence a week depending on the quality of her employer's household. Women textile operatives could receive as much as 15 shillings and ninepence a week while some clothing workers earned less than three shillings for a full week's work. (Twelve pennies made a shilling and 20 shillings a pound.)

In the months building up to the great Hyde Park meeting Emmeline toured the country speaking to crowds of up to 100,000. Her oratory was spellbinding, delivered confidently without notes, the elegant, diminutive speaker simply standing directly before her audience. The contrast between the press reports of her firebrand activism and the appearance of this refined 50-year-old in a velvet dress and a lacy blouse was the most immediately striking aspect of her performance to observers, confirming the truism that in order to be heard as a radical, it is best to dress conservatively.

The large number of by-elections that took place in the early 1900s (every ministerial move necessitated a by-election, a procedure which was later abandoned) kept Emmeline constantly on the move, from one part of the country to the next. 'Despite the public cheers she often felt herself a lonely outsider,' wrote Sylvia. 'Her life seemed harsh and joyless.'[55] At one by-election, in Newton Abbot, a group of clay-cutters who had supported the Liberal candidate and blamed Emmeline's intervention for the Conservative victory, pelted Emmeline and another woman with clay and rotten eggs. The women sought sanctuary in a grocer's shop but when they tried to escape by the back door the thugs again attacked them and Emmeline's ankle was seriously bruised. She was thrown to the ground and in danger of further assault when she made an appeal to whatever gallantry they possessed and cried out *Are none of you men?* That was enough to stop the onslaught until the police arrived.[56]

By this time Emmeline, now freed from the obligations of respectability that went with her Registrar's job, was able to go to prison for the cause. She was still limping from the attack in Newton Abbot when on 13 February 1908 she walked at the head of a group of 12 women challenging the restriction on demonstrators marching on Parliament. All were arrested and absurdly accused of 'riotous and vulgar behaviour'. Emmeline was sentenced to six weeks in prison in the 'second division', a lesson in indignity, cold and boredom that steeled her for the future. Of her time alone in a cell in the ill-ventilated Holloway prison she said: *I lay all night suffering with cold, gasping for air, aching with fatigue, and painfully wide awake.*[57]

Returning to the fray on the day of her release she arrived at a packed meeting at the Albert Hall, said to be the largest indoor women's meeting yet held. She had not been expected (she was released a day early) and made a late entrance to announce that women must do *ten times more* to win in future, for they were the natural leaders: *looking round on the muddles that men have made, looking round on the sweated and decrepit members of my sex, I say men have had the control of these things long enough, and no woman with any spark of womanliness in her will consent to let this state of things go on any longer. We are tired of it. We want to be of use; we want to have this power in order that we may try to make the world a much better place for men and women than it is today.*[58]

Emmeline's analysis was the reverse image of that offered by conservative thinkers about gender. Those who wished to deny women the vote, from both the left and right of the political spectrum, believed that men were the natural performers in the public arena and women were best suited to home life. Emmeline was propounding exactly the opposite view: that men had performed badly in the public arena and women would run matters, particularly social legislation, far better than men. While these views were different, they were clearly both predicated on a commonly held notion that gender difference was supremely important and conferred special qualities that were able to be translated into different performance in political life.

The Liberal government in the period before World War One was often wrong-footed in its reaction to the suffragettes. Home Secretary Herbert Gladstone made a strategic error when he explained the government's refusal to give time to a private member's bill brought by Liberal Henry Stanger that had received a second-reading majority of 273 to 94. Women had a fine argument for the vote, he acknowledged in the House of Commons, but 'experience shows that predominance of argument alone . . . is not enough to win the political day . . . Members of the House reflect the opinions of the country not only in regard to the numbers outside, but with regard to the intensity of feeling . . . Men have learned their lesson, and know the necessity for establishing that force majeure which actuates and arms a Government for effective work. That is the task before the supporters of this great movement . . . No doubt there is a great and growing movement in favour of granting the franchise to women, but the movement lacks numbers. Looking back at the great political crises in the thirties, the sixties and the eighties [when reform bills enfranchised successive groups of men] it will be found that people did not go about in small groups, nor were they content with enthusiastic meetings in large halls; they assembled in their tens of thousands all over the country . . . of course it is not to be expected that women could assemble in such masses, but . . . power rests with the masses and through this power a government could be influenced into more effective action . . .'[59] If women would only behave as men had done, he was saying, they could win the vote but, of course, they couldn't so behave. For Emmeline and her supporters this was tantamount to incitement. If the Home Secretary wanted to see angry women, they would give him angry women.

Clearly there should be a new militancy, but quite what it was going to be was not obvious. The implacable opponent of women's suffrage, Herbert Asquith, became Prime Minister in April 1908, following Henry Campbell-Bannerman's resignation on grounds of ill health. The great Hyde Park demonstration that June sent the Liberal leader a strong message that he should bring forward a suffrage measure but he refused to add anything to a previous equivocal statement.

Another mass demonstration in Parliament Square therefore took place on 30 June 1908. Again women attempted to make speeches outside Parliament and again they were arrested. Angry

Two suffragettes impress Herbert Asquith (left) with the importance of giving women the vote

at the rough treatment meted out to their colleagues, two women, Edith New and Mary Leigh went to Downing Street and threw stones that broke two of the new Prime Minister's windows – the first destructive militant action.

They were arrested and sent a message to Emmeline that as their action was unauthorised, she should repudiate them if she saw fit. Emmeline again showed that flash of genius that distinguished her as a leader: she visited them in the police cells and assured them of her approval for their actions. It was a portent of things to come.

In October 1908, soon after the reopening of Parliament, another demonstration was called by a leaflet summoning 'Men and Women' to 'Help the Suffragettes to Rush the House of Commons'. Emmeline, Christabel and Flora Drummond, another leading member of the WSPU, were summoned to Bow Street police station on a charge of incitement to riot. They refused to go at the appointed time but gave word that the police could come and get them at a specific time, as if they were ladies giving orders to the removal men. Thus the police had to come to their headquarters in Clement's Inn and arrest them in front of the waiting press cameras. In order to make their stay in the police cells both comfortable and much talked about, Emmeline contacted James Murray, a Liberal MP who was a sympathiser. He arranged for beds and other comforts to be sent from the Savoy Hotel and a meal to be served by three waiters on a table with flowers, silver and candlesticks. Lady Constance Lytton brought rugs and bedding to the prisoners. The judicial system was in danger of being overwhelmed by this unaccustomed behaviour. Prisoners were expected to be cowed or surly: the more proud and imperious the suffragettes were, the more difficult it was to deal with them in conventional penal style.

Christabel conducted the women's case in court. She had passed her law degree but as women were forbidden from practising in

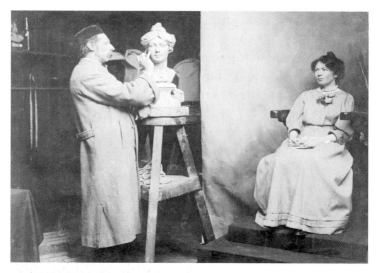
Christabel Pankhurst being modelled at Madam Tussaud's by Mr Tussaud

Britain, she had never appeared at the bar. Her request for a full jury trial was denied but she turned the proceedings into a legal spectacular by serving subpoenas on Home Secretary Herbert Gladstone and Chancellor of the Exchequer Lloyd George who were obliged to answer her questions, making the trial a fine performance for the newspapers. Emmeline finished her statement to the magistrate with the memorable line: *We are here not because we are law-breakers, we are here in our efforts to become law-makers.*[60]

The two older women were sentenced to three months' imprisonment, Christabel to ten weeks. Christabel bore her punishment less well than other suffragettes. She needed high levels of danger and excitement to raise her from torpor – technically, she was described as 'under-aroused' – and the dull monotony of prison life was particularly oppressive to her. Emmeline, on the other hand, throve on an atmosphere in which she could constantly kick against authority, browbeating the prison officers with her superior manners and dignity. She successfully refused such standard treatment as being strip-searched and having to undress in front of wardresses. She also refused to accept the restriction on speaking to her fellow prisoners. At one exercise time she called to Christabel, walked over and linked arms with her, suffragette prisoners cheered in support and troops of wardresses hustled them to the cells for three days' solitary confinement for their mutiny. Emmeline was placed in solitary confinement permanently as a 'dangerous prisoner' as she would not give an

Emmeline and Christabel posing in prison dress after their release from Holloway

assurance she would abide by the silence rule. The Home Secretary was eventually prevailed upon by repeated questions in Parliament to allow Emmeline and Christabel to meet each day and to have newspapers.

Emmeline wrote to the Home Secretary to demand the rights of a political prisoner, to have books and writing materials, her own food and clothes, to see her secretary and to associate with other suffragettes. The Home Secretary refused her demand and remarked that the suffragettes could not court a prison sentence and then, when they had received one, expect to be treated better than everyone else. He showed no imagination in this: conceding their right to be treated as political prisoners immediately and making it publicly known how well they were being treated would have undermined admiration for their martyrdom. It was at a later time, when the suffragettes contrived to make their prison sentences as demeaning and brutal as possible, that they gained the greatest sympathy.

Suffragettes outside worked to establish prison uniform as a badge of courage and imprisonment as proof of character. They demonstrated outside Holloway prison, dressed in copies of prison uniform to show solidarity, loudly singing suffragette songs so Emmeline and her colleagues could hear them over the high walls. A silver 'prison badge' was made up in Union colours to be awarded to those who had been imprisoned for the cause.

The WSPU greeted Emmeline's early release at the same time as Christabel, on 19 December 1908, with a procession in full WSPU regalia through the West End of London and a victory breakfast at the Inns of Court Hotel. At a later mass meeting in the Queen's Hall the organisers and officials of the Union lined up and saluted Emmeline and she was presented with a gold chain with a pendant of gems in WSPU colours: amethysts, pearls and agate. At the victory breakfast the gathering had sung *Rule Britannia*, a reminder that, like so many other campaigners in the Victorian and Edwardian period, the suffragettes had a clear conviction that the political system was unjust and in no way serving their interests, and just as clear a conviction that Britain was the greatest country in the world.

Emmeline had become increasingly distant from her three youngest children. Harry in particular found little place in an all-female organisation that tended to stigmatise males as the cause of all their problems. He grew up into a gentle, agreeable young man, rather dreamy but willing to help with any WSPU activity. Emmeline had difficulties appreciating his qualities and felt a dose of tough living in the fresh air would cure his physical frailty. In 1907 she sent him as an apprentice to a small builder on Clydeside. When the builder went bust, Emmeline sent Harry to work on the farm of a WSPU supporter in Essex.

Emmeline had so little sympathy with physical weakness that she seems to have been literally unable to see the illness of her children. Adela, who had become Yorkshire organiser for the WSPU, spent months organising the campaign during by-elections in Scotland and ravaged her weak constitution with outdoor work in the cold and damp. Though she was so ill she clearly had difficulty in breathing, Emmeline still sent her out, to the ire of the doctor who treated her for pneumonia. It may be that the two younger children, knowing their mother's contempt for illness, concealed it from her.

Emmeline was together with Christabel and Sylvia in Teignmouth at Christmas 1907 but Sylvia was weepy and emotional, probably because she had received a letter from Keir Hardie expressing his desire (not in fact carried through) to terminate their relationship. Sylvia would only stay a day and left on Boxing Day, feeling her mother's 'disgust' for her.[61] Did Emmeline know or guess about the relationship at this time? If she did not know now, she soon would and it would serve to intensify the distaste she already often felt for her second daughter.

Emmeline was squeamish about sex. The writer of her 'autobiography', Rheta Childe Dorr, said she 'could never get her to talk about any phase of women's sex nature. The subject repelled her. She had a strong puritan streak and thought the only solution of the social evil was the conversion of men to complete celibacy outside marriage.'[62] Yet Emmeline had enjoyed a physically demonstrative relationship with her own husband and an active sex life for at least ten years into the marriage (the conception of Harry). She had earlier talked about having a 'free union' with Richard Pankhurst without marriage and one of her closest colleagues, Elizabeth Wolstenholme, had been six months pregnant in a free union until she was persuaded to marry to damp down the scandal.

She had difficulty in contemplating sex, however. When she sent Annie Kenney to London as an organiser, Emmeline told her not to speak to any man in the street except a policeman. She urged Elizabeth Robins to alter her novel *The Convert* (which she had seen in draft) as it featured a woman who had sex outside of marriage and worked for the WSPU; Robins' play *Votes for Women* was developed from the same theme. Emmeline had Robins change the name of the character so it shared no syllables with Christabel's, and to make her a sympathiser with, rather than a member of the Union.

Christabel was curiously sexless, despite her poise and beauty. She was a queenly woman who was feared by men and idolised by other women. That she did not marry is not so remarkable but she appeared to have no boyfriends or girlfriends at all. Unlike Sylvia, she was a fine platform speaker, and unlike Harry and Adela, she was never ill. She was to Emmeline the perfect child. Stella Cobden-Sanderson said Emmeline would 'walk over the dead bodies of all her children except Christabel and say "just look what I have done for the cause".'[63] Her life as a mother was to see the loss, by one means or another, of all her children except Christabel.

Forcible Feeding Starts

By the summer of 1909 the WSPU was losing support after the great achievements of 1908. Its ability to attract backers from high society meant funds were high but the leaders had pushed the Union to the limit of display and organisation for the great demonstration of June 1908 and, whether it had in fact been half a million strong or less, the WSPU was not going to do anything better. The King's Speech of February 1909 included no mention of women's suffrage, so once again there was a women's parliament in Caxton Hall and a deputation of women again rushed Parliament and many were again arrested, including Emmeline Pethick Lawrence. At her release on 16 April a crowd greeted her and she returned to a procession led by a suffragette dressed in armour as Joan of Arc riding a white horse and flying a purple, white and green banner. Emmeline Pankhurst was offering colourful but minor variations on more of the same unsuccessful agitation.

Suffragette dressed as Joan of Arc often led processions

Worse still, despite the heroic efforts of Emmeline and her colleagues, the government was not losing by-elections. The Liberal government was extremely popular, having introduced old-age pensions in 1908, and was gearing up for a great constitutional battle, not over women's suffrage but the House of Lords. The Liberal party was riding high and could afford such potentially disastrous procedures as refusing to admit women to political meetings unless accompanied by a man, and in some cases refusing to allow women into meetings at all.

Journalist Henry Nevison described Emmeline leading a procession to Parliament to exercise the ancient right of petition on 29 June 1909: 'alone, in front of them all, walked Mrs Pankhurst, pale but proud and perfectly calm, with that look of courage and persistency on her face which I should not like my enemies to wear. The crowd received her with overwhelming enthusiasm.'[64] Asquith was not budging, however, and Emmeline received a formal note from him refusing to meet her, which she threw to the ground. When ordered to leave she forced her arrest by committing a technical assault, striking a police inspector lightly on the cheek. Police then attempted to clear the square, which resulted in the usual mass arrests. That evening in a protest against the brutal treatment of women before arrest, some 14 suffragettes stood outside the Home Office, the Treasury and other government offices and threw stones at the windows. The stones were wrapped in paper bearing messages and tied with string to reduce the chance of their hurting anyone they might inadvertently hit.

At almost the same time that window breaking was becoming a standard direct action tactic, a suffragette in Holloway began the first hunger strike. She was Marion Wallace Dunlop, an artist arrested for painting an extract from the Bill of Rights of 1689 concerning the rights of the subject to petition on the wall of St Stephen's Hall in the House of Commons. In an attempt to gain political status and to be held in the first division she went on hunger strike and was released within four days. The 14 stone-throwers also demanded first division status, refused to wear prison clothes and smashed the windows of their cells. They were put into punishment cells, went on hunger strike and were released.

All militant women were now going to go on hunger strike. The next couple to do so were Mary Leigh and Charlotte Marsh, who were given three and two months' hard labour respectively in Winson Green prison in September 1909. They had torn up slates on the roof of a house next door to where Herbert Asquith was going to speak and thrown them down on his car. This time the authorities felt they had to act. They took to 'forcibly feeding' the women, putting a rubber tube into the stomach, via the nose or mouth, and pouring liquid food through it. This grotesque procedure, alongside stories of women being forcibly stripped for refusing to wear prison regulation clothes and thrown into underground punishment cells, was making Liberal Britain look like a barbaric country that denied human rights.

Someone seized me by the head and thrust a sheet under my chin. My eyes were shut. I set my teeth and tightened my lips over them with all my strength. A man's hands were trying to force open my mouth; my breath was coming so fast that I felt as though I should suffocate. His fingers were striving to pull my lips apart – getting inside. I felt them and a steel instrument pressing round my gums, feeling for gaps in my teeth. I was trying to jerk my head away, trying to wrench it free. Two of them were holding it, two of them dragging at my mouth. I was panting and heaving, my breath quicker and louder, coming now with a low scream which was growing louder. 'Here is a gap,' one of them said. 'No, here is a better one. This long gap here!' A steel instrument pressed my gums, cutting into the flesh. I braced myself to resist that terrible pain. 'No, that won't do' – that voice again. 'Give me the pointed one!' A stab of sharp, intolerable agony. I wrenched my head free. Again they grasped me. Again the struggle. Again the steel cutting its way in, though I strained my force against it. Then something gradually forced my jaws apart as a screw was turned; the pain was like

having the teeth drawn. They were trying to get the tube down my throat, I was struggling madly to stiffen my muscles and close my throat. They got it down, I suppose, though I was unconscious of anything then save a mad revolt of struggling, for they said at last: 'That's all!' and I vomited as the tube came up. They left me on the bed exhausted, gasping for breath and sobbing convulsively.

Sylvia Pankhurst, *The Suffragette Movement*

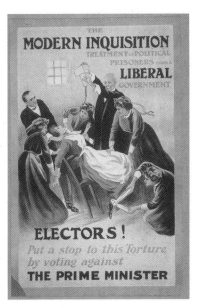

Poster protesting against forcible feeding, 1910

Emmeline had been released at the trial after her Parliament Square arrest, pending an appeal over the question of her right to petition. Five months later the Lord Chief Justice upheld her conviction by the previous court but later someone paid the fine for her and the case was discharged. She was therefore out of prison during the second half of 1909 when hunger striking, as she said, *lifted the militant movement to a new and more heroic plane*.[65] Emmeline and Christabel travelled up to Birmingham with a solicitor, unsuccessfully challenging the legality of forcible feeding. Keir Hardie denounced the procedure in the House of Commons, as did medical opinion and the press. It certainly gave a boost to the movement in terms of publicity, for newspapers had become jaded with meetings and demonstrations in Parliament Square.

Adela was in Dundee prison in the middle of October 1909, having been given a ten-day sentence along with others for attempting to disrupt Winston Churchill's meetings. She and her comrades went on hunger strike but the Scottish authorities acted with discretion in releasing them after four days of imprisonment. Prison intensified Adela's depressive nature and her feelings that her great sacrifices for the movement were unrecognised. She also felt she was being supplanted in her mother's affections by the more compliant Annie Kenney.

If Emmeline had any concerns about Adela at this time they were subsumed under more urgent considerations about Harry. He had been struck down with an inflammation of the spinal cord and was paralysed from the waist down. In fact he had poliomyelitis, though this was not appreciated at the time. Emmeline was stunned, particularly as she was planning to leave in a few days' time for a lecture tour on the lucrative North American circuit. Harry was taken from the farm in Essex where he had been working to the Pembridge Gardens nursing home in London where Emmeline visited and consulted medical staff.

They reassured her he would improve with time and rest. She had to decide whether to go off on the tour and, as anyone who knew her would have predicted, decided to go. 'So ruthless was the inner call to action', as Sylvia said, 'there was never a moment of doubt as to where she would be substituted – on the platform or by the bedside of her son.'[66] Some have attributed Sylvia's words to bitterness but they offer an accurate description of the campaigners' all-surpassing passion for the cause. Sylvia made this clearer in her biography of her mother, writing that she 'steeled herself to persevere with her journey, declaring that he would recover as before'.[67] She also needed to make money, particularly now, as nursing care was expensive.

In recognition of her celebrity status Emmeline was given the best cabin on the White Star Line for the standard fare. She spent some eight weeks in the USA and Canada, giving lectures that won over the audience immediately with characteristic humour. The refined 50-year-old woman would begin in a low tone: 'I am what you call a hooligan.'[68] She received widespread support from women's suffrage supporters and grudging respect from opponents.

The burden of caring for Harry had fallen to Sylvia, who told Emmeline after her return on 8 December 1909 that Harry would never walk again. *He would be better dead*, Emmeline said, a telling indication of her visceral disgust at physical illness.[69]

Harry had previously suffered from a severe inflammation of the bladder. Now the condition returned, and in his weakened state doctors knew he would not withstand it. They gave him weeks to live. Sylvia spent long hours talking to Harry and learned that he had fallen in love with Helen Craggs, a full-time employee of the WSPU who — he had met while campaigning the previous year. While Emmeline was still in America, Sylvia had Helen sent for and he was able to enjoy time in his last weeks with a woman he loved. Sylvia was sensitive to the needs of love but Emmeline resented her action, saying Helen was 'taking from her the last of her son' and blaming Sylvia for bringing Helen in.[70] Harry died on 5 January 1910 and was buried at Highgate cemetery where his brother was also buried. Emmeline said she wanted to be buried there, telling Sylvia, *when my time comes, I want to be put with my two boys.*

Harry Pankhurst

Sylvia said her mother at the funeral was 'broken as I had never seen her; huddled together without a care for her appearance, she seemed an old, plain and cheerless woman.'[71] She was due to take a train to speak in the north that evening, and did so to an audience who knew of her bereavement. They would have understood had she chosen not to proceed, but their respect for her was the greater because she went ahead, putting the cause before her personal feelings, as she always expected others to do.

The Argument of the Stone: 1910–1912

The mass activities for which the suffragettes are most remembered – hunger strikes and breaking windows – were not the invention of Emmeline or even of other WSPU leaders but of individual members responding to a general incitement to action. Emmeline's genius was to recognise the effectiveness of particular sporadic acts of militancy and mark them out as future WSPU policy. She was also adept at interpreting protests in a way that minimised the element of mere criminal damage and showed the authorities in the worst possible light. The day-to-day direction of militant actions was under Christabel's control.

The hunger strikes and forcible feeding of 1909 shocked both the suffragettes and the authorities. They also brought class distinctions into sharp focus. Working-class Mary Leigh was forcibly fed while Lady Constance Lytton was freed. Ashamed of this preferential treatment, Lady Lytton had herself re-arrested in the guise of a working-class woman and was forcibly fed eight times before release, enabling the WSPU to gain publicity from the aristocratic glamour of Lady Lytton as well as showing up the class bias of the prison system.

One suffragette, Charlotte Marsh, was forcibly fed 139 times. Clearly the authorities were prepared to go on with the procedure and, after the initial publicity, the WSPU was making no political gains for its members' pain. Emmeline declared a truce on 31 January 1910. The suffering was too great and too pointless, and there were signs the government would grant concessions if they could do so without appearing to yield to coercion. The fatigue of bereavement must also have played a part. The

WSPU was so closely connected to one family that the family's tragedy affected policy for the whole movement.

Emmeline felt able to suspend the Union's militancy because of an important initiative by Henry Brailsford, a senior journalist who had resigned from the *Daily News* in protest at the editor's support for force-feeding. A general election of January 1910 had returned the Liberals but with a greatly reduced majority. In the altered political climate following the election Brailsford set up a body to be known as the Conciliation Committee chaired by Lord Lytton, a Conservative peer and brother of the suffragette. The committee included MPs of all parties and aimed to put forward a compromise bill for women's suffrage. Though the bill had good intentions, it tended to be seen as partisan because its provisions were generally in line with the Conservative party's wish to enfranchise the propertied class: it gave the vote to female heads of household and occupiers of property with a £10 rentable value. All the suffrage societies supported it, though many without enthusiasm.

Labour MP David Shackleton's Women's Franchise (Conciliation) Bill was introduced a month after a widely supported demonstration of 18 June 1910 that included a prisoners' pageant of more than 600 women who had gone to prison for the cause, led by Emmeline herself. The Bill passed its second reading by a large majority, but the government then sent it to a 'committee of the whole house', which meant that unless the government would give it time, it must fail.

Herbert Henry Asquith (1852–1928) was the son of a Yorkshire clothing manufacturer. Educated at City of London School and Balliol College Oxford, he became a barrister before being elected as Liberal MP for East Fife in 1886. He was ambitious, clever and a fine speaker. He became Home Secretary under Gladstone in 1892, and then again under Rosebery. Out of office for a decade from 1895 when the Conservatives took over, he was made Chancellor of the Exchequer in the new Liberal government of 1905. He introduced higher taxes on unearned income, which helped pay for pensions for the over-70s. In 1908 he became Prime Minister following the resignation of Henry Campbell-Bannerman and won an election in early 1910. When the Lords rejected his Chancellor David Lloyd George's budget it led to open conflict between the two Houses of Parliament that culminated in the 'Peers vs the People' election of December 1910, after which Asquith had a majority, with the help of Labour and Irish MPs. The Liberals were then able to pass the Parliament Act, curtailing the power of the Lords, and the National Insurance Act, which provided insurance cover for unemployment and illness. As Prime Minister, Asquith presided over a period of national upheaval. Irish Home Rule, labour unrest and women's suffrage dominated the political scene. He took Britain into World War One but he proved a poor war leader. Lloyd George, in alliance with the Conservatives, eventually forced Asquith to resign in December 1916.

Asquith was hostile to female suffrage. Some have suggested that the behaviour of his indiscreet, socially ambitious wife Margot Tennant, who so liked to meddle in politics that he took to refusing to tell her anything, led him to believe women were psychologically unsuited to public life.

H H Asquith caricatured by Spy

Asquith informed Lord Lytton on 23 July, the day of a massive peaceful suffrage demonstration in Hyde Park, that the Conciliation Bill would not be granted further time that session.

So much for conciliation. Emmeline restrained her militants, however, and kept up the truce, in the hope that subtle pressure would encourage the government to find time for the bill in the following parliament commencing in autumn.

At a giant meeting in the Albert Hall on 10 November, Emmeline threatened an end to the truce. Parliament was due to be dissolved on 28 November for the 'People vs the Peers' election, as the

'Black Friday' A Suffragette lies injured outside the Houses of Parliament, 18 November 1910

government was locked in conflict with the House of Lords. Emmeline had already said: *If the Conciliation Bill is killed, there will be an end to our truce.*[72] She was speaking to a meeting at the Caxton Hall on 18 November when the news came through that no provision was to be made for anything but government business in the days remaining. Nothing was said of the Conciliation Bill.

Emmeline immediately divided the audience into contingents of 12 for a march on Parliament. Emmeline and Elizabeth Garrett Anderson were allowed through but others in the first group were driven back and Emmeline watched in horror for hours as police used force to beat the women back. She described how the police *laid hands on the women and literally threw them from one man to another. Some of the police used their fists, striking the women in their faces, their breast, their shoulders. One woman I saw thrown down with violence three or four times in rapid succession . . . {it was} unanimous and wholesale brutality.*[73]

The Home Secretary, Winston Churchill, had decided that there was little point in arresting women then having to deal with criticism of their treatment in prison, particularly as they considered imprisonment a badge of courage. Police had therefore been instructed not to make arrests but to use all force necessary to stop the women's advance.

Churchill's tactics were sound in theory but did not take into account the feelings of the men themselves, given the freedom to physically manhandle women. Many officers doubtless showed restraint, but comment after what came to be called 'Black Friday' focused on physical assaults on the women including sexual assaults consisting of wrenching breasts and lifting skirts. The presence of plain-clothes police in the crowd and men who joined in to take the opportunity of assaulting women with impunity added to the confusion.

After six hours of battle, police arrested 119 suffragettes but released all of them the next day. The following Tuesday, when Asquith had said he would give a statement on women's suffrage, the sequence of events was repeated on a smaller scale. News came through to a suffragette meeting at the Caxton Hall that Asquith had said the Conciliation Bill would be given facilities in the next parliament. Next parliament was not enough for the suffragettes, they wanted the next session of this parliament, as soon as the House was meeting again, and also questioned the good faith of the Prime Minister.

I am going to Downing Street. Come along, all of you said Emmeline.[74] She and her contingent walked directly into the police cordon and were subjected to similar violence and arrests. Emmeline was also arrested this time and taken to Cannon Row police station where her sister Mary tried to visit her that evening. When she was not allowed to do so, she threw a stone through the window and was arrested, as were a number of other militants who sought out the homes of cabinet ministers and threw stones at the windows.

Non-militant suffrage campaigners in the National Union of Women's Suffrage Societies were infuriated that Emmeline's movement had broken their truce when there was still life in the Conciliation Bill. To Emmeline's contemporary critics, this went to the heart of Emmeline's weaknesses. She was too petulant, too mistrustful of the authorities, as if only she knew what was going on and everything the authorities said was a lie. As Lord Lytton said to a meeting: 'Conciliation and militancy cannot go hand in hand. What is so humiliating in this fresh outbreak is that it implies that the committee has failed, and we have not failed. The committee has accepted on good faith the Prime Minister's statement as an undertaking to grant facilities to our Bill in the next parliament.'[75]

Emmeline's mother died in spring 1910, aged 75, and there was another personal tragedy in store for Emmeline that year. Her sister Mary's health had been poor. She should not have been putting herself in danger on Black Friday or courting arrest later, but the ethic of the WSPU demanded personal sacrifice for the cause: the greater the sacrifice, the more highly it was regarded. Mary was welcomed back from Holloway with a lunch for herself and the other released prisoners presided over by Emmeline; a few days later the sisters celebrated Christmas Day together at their brother Herbert's house with other members of the family. Mary quietly left the table at lunch,

Mary Clarke, Emmeline's sister and a substitute mother to her children

saying she wanted to lie down. When Emmeline went to see her upstairs she was already dying from a stroke.

After Harry's, this second death of a close relative within a year hit the family hard. Sylvia had not spent Christmas with the family and Emmeline had to go to her studio to tell her of Mary's death. 'Stunned by our sorrow, we clung together,' Sylvia said.[76] Mary had been a mother to Adela during Emmeline's long absences so she felt the loss particularly.

Emmeline put her grief aside to campaign in the general election. The Asquith government was again returned with an only slightly reduced majority. An MP who had drawn first place in the ballot for private members' bills resurrected the Conciliation Bill and the truce was renewed. The bill now related only to women with a household qualification so it was a proposal to enfranchise a small number but it still enjoyed Emmeline's support. Asked in America that summer 'When will English women vote?' she replied: *Next year.*[77]

In May 1911, like its predecessor, the bill passed its second reading with a large majority. The principle of women's suffrage had again clearly been won; it remained only to establish the exact terms. In a spirit of reconciliation the WSPU joined with 28 other suffrage societies in a procession to mark the coronation of George V as a response from 'the King's loyal subjects' to the official processions, which were to be almost entirely male.

Behind the scenes the Conciliation Bill was running into trouble. Its apparently sunny prospects had alerted members of Liberal associations to its implications for the future political picture and the old problem arose. Emmeline wanted the franchise to be a gender issue: for women to have the vote on the same basis as men. For the party apparatchiks it was always a political issue: for whom would the next block of people to be enfranchised be most likely to vote? It seemed obvious that hundreds of thousands of householder votes would be more likely to

Indian suffragettes on the Women's Coronation Procession, London, June 1911

strengthen the Conservative party. The Liberals had suffered 20 years of political impotence following the split over Irish Home Rule. Now they were back with a majority. Were they going to hand it over to the Tories? Lloyd George, a supporter of women's suffrage, was working behind the scenes against the Conciliation Bill to build up support amongst the Liberals for extended franchise legislation that would put working-class men and women on the electoral register as well as property owners.

Unsurprisingly, Lloyd George won the argument. Emmeline was in the US on another lecture tour when she received the news that on 7 November 1911 Asquith had announced the next session would include a government manhood suffrage bill. He added that the bill would be open to amendment and the government would not oppose an amendment about women's suffrage, but for Emmeline it was a betrayal. The Conciliation Bill was based on existing franchise laws: a change in those laws would destroy it. *Protest imperative!* she cabled across the Atlantic.[78]

Christabel (centre) and Sylvia (right) seeing their mother off on a lecture tour of North America in 1911

The resumption of militancy was organised and swift. Women with stones and hammers smashed the widows of government offices and the National Liberal Federation. For the first time they also targeted private property: the offices of the *Daily Mail*, Swan and Edgar's and other businesses. The rank and file of the WSPU, angered at the assaults they had suffered on Black Friday and at other protests, urged a policy of stone-throwing. It was a way of making a protest and either escaping by running away or undergoing immediate arrest (and therefore not being manhandled as they had been while demonstrating).

When Emmeline returned to Britain she praised the leadership that in her absence had so decisively resumed and even stepped up militant action. In the same spirit she announced in February 1912 at a dinner to welcome the release of stonethrowers from prison that, other arguments having failed to persuade, the next argument would be that of the stone: *If the argument of the stone, that time-honoured political argument, is sufficient, then we will never use any stronger argument. And that is the weapon and the argument that we are going to use next time.* Thus she heralded a strategy of ever-increasing militancy.[79]

On Trial for Conspiracy

The WSPU's determination to control the streets with dramatic actions and their continual escalation of violence against property stimulated fierce criticism from erstwhile supporters.

Emmeline's former colleague Teresa Billington-Greig wrote three articles in *New Age*, later to be published in book form, denouncing 'emancipation in a hurry'. She wrote: 'now violence is openly advocated – but only the small violences which can be effectively contrasted with the greater ones committed by the Government. This is not advance; it is the search for a new thrill for the public and a new chain for the women who pay the price.' She looked forward with horror to the more violent action now threatened as it would 'condemn a large number of women to personal sacrifice that in some cases amounts to suicide, and in all cases to the suffering of terrible strain and much possible abuse.' The leaders were advocating 'a policy of wrecking, the deliberate choice of delay and warfare'.[80]

She offered a withering denunciation of the WSPU leadership who 'impose a yoke of emotional control by which the very virtues of the members are exploited; they produce a system of mental and spiritual slavery. The women who succumb to it exhibit a type of self-subjection not less objectionable than the more ordinary self-subjugation of women to men, to which it bears a close relation.'[81]

Emmeline stimulated both fierce antagonism and sentimental attachments, such as she had with the composer Ethel Smyth, who wrote the music for the suffragette anthem *March of the*

Women. Smyth, who was prone to sudden, passionate engagements with women, fell for Emmeline immediately, describing her at their first meeting in 1910 as 'A graceful woman, rather under middle height, one would have said a delicate woman, if the well-knit figure, the quick deft movement, the soft bright eyes that on occasion could emit lambent flame had not betokened excellent health . . . Her personality and style of speaking swept me off my feet at once. I knew that

Emmeline's friend Ethel Smyth composed the Suffragette anthem

before long I should become her slave . . .'[82] Smyth decided to devote two years of her life to the suffrage cause and became Emmeline's closest companion.

Her remarks to 'dearest Em', 'My treasure and my pride' were characteristic of ordinary affection between women at the time. When she wrote 'I lie awake at night sometimes and see you like Atlas, bearing up the world of women on your head' the hyperbole is typical of the adoration Emmeline inspired among women eager for hero-worship.[83] Smyth provided Emmeline with much needed companionship and, in her house in Surrey, a home to go to in the demanding years of 1910–12. It is difficult to decipher the nature of their relationship. Smyth wrote: 'I think it is the crowning achievement of my life to have made you love me. And proof of your cleverness to have found me – and found a new gift in yourself – the friendship you give me. Yes, I also am getting more and more "off" men.'[84] Such words are open to interpretation but, given Emmeline's fastidious nature and mistrust of the physical, it seems likely that the love between them was expressed only in chaste embraces.

On 1 March 1912 Emmeline and two others took a taxi to Downing Street and broke two windows, at which they were arrested. Throughout the day 'Mrs Pankhurst's bold, bad ones' were involved in smashing plate-glass windows in the West End.[85] Well-dressed, harmless-looking groups of women with no obvious connection to the WSPU approached major department stores and produced hammers from muffs or bags, which they used to smash plate-glass windows. Almost 400 were smashed, for which 121 women were arrested.

Frederick Pethick Lawrence bailed out Emmeline along with the others – his usual role in these affairs. Ethel Smyth had had to tutor Emmeline in throwing stones, so alien to her nature was the activity. At her first try the stone had fallen backwards out of her hand, endangering Ethel's dog. Emmeline's ineptitude in acts of vandalism perhaps lends credence to the view of C E H Hobhouse, Chancellor of the Duchy of Lancaster, who had remarked early in 1912 that 'in the case of the suffrage demand there has not been the kind of popular sentimental uprising which accounted for the arson and violence of earlier suffrage reforms.'[86] To have a cabinet minister implying that the suffragettes were insufficiently violent was a gift to the militants in the movement. Such violence was not natural to most of the suffragettes. The shift from presenting themselves in situations where they could be grappled with and beaten, to ones in which they were the aggressors went to the heart of the divisions that now tore through the suffrage movement.

Total numbers of members were not revealed but historian Martin Pugh comments that the WSPU's branches represented only one in six of the total number of women's suffrage organisations in the country.[87] The other suffrage societies felt there was the chance of real progress in 1912. An extended franchise was on the agenda; the last thing they wanted was vandalism that discredited the cause. The manhood suffrage bill under discussion – if amended to include measures for women's suffrage – would almost certainly have enfranchised more women than the Conciliation Bill. However, the suggestion was for a women's adjunct to a men's bill and that offended Emmeline's sensibilities. She was suspicious of the motives of Asquith and his government, and feared that this was a devious way of evading the issue of women's suffrage altogether. For the first time Asquith received a women's delegation, composed of all the suffrage societies. Certainly the Prime Minister would have preferred no women's franchise measure at all, but he was looking for the best deal he could get.

The WSPU's tactics were also questionable. Almost all the targets for the new militancy were shops, damage to which would not affect the government except indirectly; attacking government offices would have made a more obvious point. One reason was that shops were less well protected than government buildings and women could loiter unobtrusively around them. Perhaps, however, it is also worth remembering that Emmeline had run a shop in the West End that failed, to her great disappointment. At the least, the experience does not seem to have increased her sympathy for shopkeepers.

The Union resumed its attacks in an atmosphere made bitterer by industrial unrest, including strikes broken by troops, and resistance to an Irish Home Rule settlement from a defiant Ulster. While the suffragettes were not reaching the levels of violence to be seen in Ireland, they found wry amusement in the government that was never going to succumb to militant measures doing exactly that in Ireland. If militant measures were counter-productive, as the National Union of Women's Suffrage Societies claimed, why was the government cringing before their adoption by the Ulstermen?

Suffragette volunteers at work in the WSPU office at Clement's Inn

Four days after the West End window-breaking spree, there was another in Knightsbridge and other west London shopping streets. The next day, 5 March 1912, police raided the WSPU headquarters in Clement's Inn and seized documents. They went through every desk and every file looking for evidence of conspiracy and took Emmeline's private papers, including photographs of her children in infancy and letters from her husband, some of which she was never to see again.

The police had a warrant for the arrest of the Union's leaders for conspiracy to commit malicious damage but Emmeline was already in prison, serving two months for the window smashing and Christabel by now had her own flat and no longer lived with the Pethick Lawrences at Clement's Inn. Frederick Pethick Lawrence dispatched a messenger to warn her.

Christabel fled to a nursing home in Pembridge Gardens run by a supporter, Catherine Pine, where she was dressed as a nurse. The following day she took the boat train to Folkestone under an assumed name and fled to Paris, the start of more than two years of exile. With the other leaders in prison, Annie Kenney took charge of the Union, making weekly trips to see Christabel in France. Sylvia, who had just returned from a three-month speaking tour of the United States, expected to take over the reins of the movement but Christabel rebuffed her – one more stage in the destruction of their relationship.

This was a fateful moment. Emmeline could have insisted that Sylvia should lead but she deferred to Christabel's decision, so the Union was decapitated as the authorities had intended. Christabel, now more than ever reliant on the WSPU's rich donors, found Sylvia's socialism unattractive. Emmeline shared this feeling but there must also be a suspicion that Sylvia's active sexuality repulsed Emmeline, a revulsion that she disguised as fear that the movement would be tainted by sexual scandal if Sylvia's affair with Hardie became known.

In Holloway one wing was given over to Emmeline and the other suffragettes who enjoyed a fairly lax regime of free association and were able to amuse themselves. She emerged from Holloway to see the bitterness of non-militant suffragists: the Conciliation Bill had been rejected on its second reading. The Liberals could claim they had rejected it in favour of the government's manhood suffrage bill with the possibility of a women's suffrage amendment. Worse still, the Conservatives had voted against it in greater numbers this time than previously, even though the alternative manhood suffrage bill would do them no good electorally. It seemed that the WSPU's militant tactics had actually undermined support for women's suffrage.

Emmeline's trial for conspiracy, along with Emmeline and Frederick Pethick Lawrence and others, began on 15 May 1912. Emmeline, a conventional woman in so many ways, refused to give her age at the start of the trial and during the six-day trial gave her usual defiant account of the injustice of the law, the alleviation of the sufferings of the poor that would result from an extension of the franchise to women, and how it was not she and her co-defendants who had conspired, but the government that had conspired against those actively seeking the vote. The prosecution, led by Attorney-General Sir Rufus Isaacs, used evidence from the leaflets and circulars that the WSPU had produced to promote window-breaking and the conspiratorial coded language the suffragettes used among themselves when involved in militancy.

The jury found the defendants guilty but asked for clemency. The judge ignored the request. All three were sent down for nine months in the second division, Frederick Pethick Lawrence to the lonely confines of Brixton Prison, which saw few fighting for the women's cause, and Emmeline and Emmeline Pethick Lawrence to a heroines' welcome at Holloway.

Immediately after the celebrations for their welcome had finished, Emmeline set about lobbying for political status and so to be raised to the first division. Emmeline and Mrs Pethick Lawrence were placed in the first division and allowed comfortable chairs, their own clothes, bedding, towels and books. Ethel Smyth sent a crate of Château Lafite to Emmeline on the basis that drinking it was necessary for her health. Emmeline was delighted to have so quickly won the argument that they were political prisoners but was dismayed to find that the transfer was for leaders only, not rank-and-file militants. When the government refused to give political prisoner status to all suffragettes, they all went on hunger strike, including the leaders.

The actual hunger pangs last only about twenty-four hours with most prisoners. I generally suffer most on the second day. After that there is no very desperate craving for food. Weakness and mental depression take its place. Great disturbances of digestion divert the desire for food to a longing for relief from pain. Often there is intense headache, with fits of dizziness, or slight delirium. Complete exhaustion and a feeling of isolation from earth mark the final stages of the ordeal. Recovery is often protracted, and entire recovery of normal health is sometimes discouragingly slow.

Emmeline Pankhurst,
My Own Story

Three days into the strike forcible feeding commenced. Emmeline found it unbearable to hear the force-feeding of her comrades, saying later: *Sickening scenes of violence took place every hour of the day, as the doctors went from cell to cell performing their hideous office . . . I shall never while I live forget the suffering I experienced during the days when those cries were ringing on my ears.*[88] Finally they came to Emmeline Pethick Lawrence, Emmeline helped her to resist but she was dragged into her own cell, next door to Emmeline's.

Emmeline listened in horror to the force-feeding of 45-year-old Mrs Pethick Lawrence, who had a gastric complaint that was exacerbated by prison food at the best of times. Emmeline knew it would be her turn next. When the doctor and wardresses came to her cell door she picked up a heavy earthenware ewer from a table and threatened them: *If any of you dare take a step inside this cell, I shall defend myself.*[89] They desisted, knowing she would soon be too weak from hunger to resist further.

She consented to be medically examined, resulting in a report on her neurosis, insomnia and mental stress caused by the changes of the menopause and several days of starvation. She was easily declared a health risk, as was Emmeline Pethick Lawrence, and both were released on 24 June 1912.

Frederick Pethick Lawrence had also mounted a hunger strike, an action all the braver for his lack of supporting comrades. He had endured repeated forcible feeding – 'an unpleasant and painful process', as he described it.[90] He had lost four stones in weight when he was discharged three days after his wife and Emmeline. Within four months Emmeline was to turn on the Pethick Lawrences.

Expelling the Pethick Lawrences

Adela Pankhurst felt the WSPU's aggressive strategy was losing it ground. Calls to militancy did not take into account local conditions, of which she as a regional organiser was only too well aware. Direct action was more popular in London than the provinces and often those who wanted to see action went to London for it. Adela's protestations were ignored or misunderstood as malevolent attacks on Christabel.

Adela's health, always fragile, had been troubling her and in 1911 she seemed headed for another breakdown. Emmeline advised she relinquish her post as WSPU organiser for Sheffield and go to college to study what she wanted, though not in London, for she feared the excitement of the women's movement would not be conducive to her peace of mind. Whether for her own good or not, Emmeline was keeping Adela, now 26 years old, away from the leadership of the movement. It was the first stage in a process of effective expulsion.

Sylvia noted that though Adela was 'a brilliant speaker, and one of the hardest workers in the movement, she was often regarded with more disapproval than approbation' by her mother and Christabel.[91] Adela would probably have preferred to be enjoying the companionship and excitement of the head office, particularly if she had the longed-for approval of her mother, but she announced that she wanted to become a gardener. Emmeline said she would send her to the Studley Agricultural College in Warwickshire.

VOTES FOR WOMEN.

Miss ADELA PANKHURST,

Organiser, National Women's
Social and Political Union,
4, Clement's Inn, Strand, W.C.

Emmeline's youngest daughter Adela, one of the most gifted WSPU speakers, was kept away from the centre of power.

The choice of gardening was an odd one. It was not something in which Adela had shown an interest previously. Campaigning outdoors had done damage to her health and the salubrious effects of fresh air were more a subject associated with her mother's attitudes than hers. Regardless of that, her future was set. There was one condition: she should not speak in public again. This was doubtless also presented as a health measure, as Adela had suffered from pleurisy and a complete loss of voice and had been advised to rest from speaking. However, a permanent ban served Emmeline and Christabel's interests. They had been appalled by the left-wing slant of Adela's work in the north; Adela was opposed to the increasingly violent tactics of the Union. Emmeline and Christabel had been forging a movement which was not so much a mass representative body as a cadre of active revolutionaries supported by the donations of the rich who sometimes took part in militancy themselves but more often enjoyed the thrill of vicarious excitement. The rich donors must not be alienated, particularly with the movement's activities curtailed and Christabel living in France on donations. Her whereabouts were disclosed in September 1912 when the *Daily Sketch* was invited to take exclusive photographs of her, smartly dressed and apparently enjoying life in Paris.

The Pethick Lawrences shared the feelings of many that the Union's increasing militancy was alienating support and not advancing the cause. After their release from imprisonment they stopped off at Boulogne to meet with Emmeline and Christabel to discuss the future direction of the movement. Mrs Pethick Lawrence described their conversation: 'Henceforward [Emmeline] said there was to be a widespread attack upon public and private property, secretly carried out by suffragettes who would not offer themselves for arrest but wherever possible would make good their escape. As our minds had been moving in quite another direction, this project came as a shock to us both. We considered it sheer madness to throw away the immense publicity and propaganda value that the demonstration followed by the State trial had brought to our cause.'[92]

Frederick argued that attacks on private property such as shops were an escalation of militancy that promoted a new opposition and the public needed to be guided to a better understanding of the reason for such violence. Christabel argued that repeated and intensified militancy would itself be educative and earlier forms of militancy had also produced opposition but had been understood with time. Frederick later recalled that 'Mrs Pankhurst, as a born rebel, was even more emphatic than Christabel that the time had come to take sterner measures. She appeared to resent the fact that I had even ventured to question the wisdom of her daughter's policy.'[93]

The Pethick Lawrences went off on a holiday in Europe and Canada. While they were away the Home Office made the first moves towards making individuals responsible for WSPU activities. The government claimed the costs of the conspiracy trial from Frederick Pethick Lawrence and compensation for the shopkeepers whose windows were broken. The Treasury solicitors eventually sold his house and made him bankrupt. Emmeline had never liked Frederick. Now his vulnerability to attack by the government, coupled with the Pethick Lawrences' reluctance to proceed further down the path of militancy, gave Emmeline the opportunity she required.

The first the Pethick Lawrences knew of Emmeline's intentions was a letter saying that the authorities and insurance companies could attack Pethick Lawrence and thus weaken the movement. As Sylvia recorded it: 'Mr Pethick Lawrence, once a great asset to the Union, had become a disability in her eyes.'[94] Emmeline Pethick Lawrence said, 'She urged us to remain in Canada and make our domicile there and to remove our private property from our bank in London to safety beyond the reach of confiscation by the government . . . we wrote in reply that having staked our health and life on the vindication of the principle of human equality, we could not renounce it because of a risk to our property.'[95]

When the Pethick Lawrences stepped off the boat back in England they were met by a friend on the dock who said: 'They are going to turn you out of the Women's Social and Political Union.'[96] The Union had moved as the lease had run out and, at the new headquarters at Lincoln's Inn House, the returning couple found they had no offices, conversations ceased as they approached, and Annie Kenney even refused to speak to Mrs Pethick Lawrence. Emmeline called them into her office and told them they would be expelled. The Pethick Lawrences could not believe what she was saying. In particular they could not accept that Christabel, who had lived as a member of their family for six years and was particularly adored by Frederick, could have acquiesced in this. Christabel therefore briefly flitted in from her exile, heavily disguised, and took part in a meeting in London at which Annie Kenney, Emmeline Pethick Lawrence's favourite, was also present to emphasise the united front against them. The fact that Emmeline Pankhurst would risk Christabel's safety for the expulsion shows how dedicated she was to removing her old colleagues, who owned the newspaper *Votes for Women* and were guarantors for the lease on the new head office building.

The Pethick Lawrences faced their fate with dignity. Frederick noted the irony that 'There was . . . no appeal against our expulsion from the WSPU. Mrs Pankhurst was the acknowledged autocrat of the Union. We had ourselves supported her in acquiring this position several years previously; we could not dispute it now.'[97] It was in the interest of all for the split to proceed with the minimum disruption to the cause they all favoured, so the Pethick Lawrences accepted the *fait accompli*. They were shocked to find that Christabel had already set up a replacement newspaper, *The Suffragette*, ready to print as soon as they were ousted. The Pankhursts had clearly been planning for their removal. The Pethick Lawrences were not present at the meeting at the Albert Hall called to celebrate the release of the conspiracy trial prisoners. Emmeline was alone congratulated. 'From then on I never saw or heard from Mrs Pankhurst again,' wrote Emmeline Pethick Lawrence, 'and Christabel, who had shared our family life, became a complete stranger. The Pankhursts did nothing by halves.'[98]

Frederick Pethick Lawrence summed up the Pankhurst character: 'The one outstanding characteristic which they [Emmeline and Christabel] shared with one another . . . was their absolute refusal to be deflected by criticism or appeal one hair's breadth from the course which they had determined to pursue. To that extent they were insensitive to ordinary human considerations. Many men and women who have made history have been cast in a similar mould.'[99]

The damage the split had done was not immediately obvious. The Pethick Lawrences formed a rival group, the United Suffragists, but it did not aspire to be a mass movement like the Women's Freedom League formed after the 1907 split. However, Emmeline's behaviour towards the Pethick Lawrences did lose the WSPU some of its most influential supporters. The loss of Frederick and Emmeline Pethick Lawrence also meant the loss of the best financial and managerial brains in the Union. Emmeline Pankhurst tried to redress this by herself taking the place of treasurer, a position for which she was not suited in practical or emotional terms and for which, with her speaking engagements, she had no time. The Union's accounting tumbled into disorder at a time when increased militancy meant a firm hand was required and the Union's finances and those of the Pankhurst family became ever more confused.

Days after the expulsion, speaking at the Albert Hall, Emmeline made a renewed call for militancy: *Be militant each in your own way . . . Those of you who can break windows – break them. Those of you who can still further attack the sacred idol of property so as to make the Government realise that property is as greatly endangered by women's suffrage as it was by the Chartists of old days – do so.*[100] In a contemporary reference, she taunted the government that she was inciting the meeting to rebellion at a time when they dared not indict the Ulstermen for their blatant incitement.

The militancy was indeed to be extreme, for those with a taste for it. Christabel had already told Sylvia to burn down Nottingham Castle.

Guerrilla Warfare: 1912–1913

Once a decision had been taken to attack private property, arson was an obvious strategy to adopt as an escalation of militancy, though its first practitioners were rank-and-file members acting on their own initiative. Emily Wilding Davison, a Union member but one who conceived and enacted her plans alone, first set fire to the mail in pillar boxes using a rag soaked in paraffin in December 1911.

The sentence of six months did not deter Helen Craggs, girlfriend of the doomed Harry Pankhurst, who was caught in the garden of Nuneham House, home of Colonial Secretary Lewis Harcourt on 13 July 1912 with inflammable oil and other incendiary materials. Emmeline had not known of this in advance, but when Craggs was sent down for nine months Emmeline repeated her assertion that she would never repudiate or disown anyone fighting for the cause.

Gladys Evans and Mary Leigh later tried to burn down the Theatre Royal in Dublin. While the audience was dispersing they poured petrol on the curtains of a box and set fire to them, and threw a flaming chair over the edge into the orchestra. Again, Emmeline had not known of the intended arson in advance but called it an *outrageous act of reprisal* when a five year sentence was passed on Evans and Leigh *whom we love and honour for their splendid courage.*[101]

Arson is treated with utmost seriousness by the law because fire is so uncontrollable: it often leads to loss of life, including that of fire-fighters, regardless of the intention of the arsonist. Emmeline was either not aware of the dangers or not concerned about them. She had said in the past that the next step after window-breaking was *incendiarism*. After the expulsion of the Pethick Lawrences, the focus of the WSPU splintered, with the Union's members falling into sporadic acts of violence. Keir Hardie wrote that Emmeline had made 'a grave error of judgement' in the way she chose to fight the women's case, though this was in a private letter; in public he showed solidarity.[102]

Our task was to show the Government that it was expedient to yield to the women's just demands. In order to do that we had to make England and every department of English life insecure and unsafe. We had to make English law a failure and the courts farce comedy theatres; we had to discredit the Government and Parliament in the eyes of the world; we had to spoil English sports, hurt business, destroy valuable property, demoralise the world of society, shame the churches, upset the whole orderly conduct of life – That is, we had to do as much of this guerilla warfare as the people of England would tolerate.

Emmeline Pankhurst,
My Own Story

Adela had previously made clear her opposition to these extremes of violence. Now Sylvia too gave voice. She had restrained her criticism of the Union, instead arguing positively that the WSPU must be part of a mass movement that involved working-class women. She later wrote that she 'regarded this new policy with grief and regret, believing it wholly mistaken and unnecessary, deeply deploring the life of furtive destruction it would impose on the participators, and the harsh punishment it was preparing for them.'[103] Sylvia was shocked to receive the message from Christabel to burn down Nottingham Castle. 'The idea,' she wrote, 'of doing such a stealthy deed of destruction was repugnant. I did not think such an act could assist the cause.'[104] The most Sylvia would agree to was a torchlight procession to the castle.

Sylvia moved to the East End, where the tradition of feminist and working-class activism gave fertile ground for her form of militancy. Her campaigning in the East End influenced the Labour

MP George Lansbury, who demonstrated that sacrifice was not limited to women alone by resigning his seat of Bromley and Bow over the Labour party's lukewarm support for women's suffrage. He stood as an Independent and Emmeline campaigned for him, the first WSPU-sponsored candidate, but he lost his seat to the Conservatives in November 1912. Henceforward the Union did not even pretend to seek electoral legitimacy or work within the parliamentary system.

The manhood suffrage bill was going through Parliament with women's suffrage amendments through most of 1912 and the National Union of Women's Suffrage Societies urged the suffragettes to suspend militancy so as not to jeopardise its chances. Eventually Emmeline urged her supporters to desist from militancy so the WSPU would not be blamed for the failure of the bill, though this was merely a hiatus: they had no confidence in the ability of the parliamentary system to deliver the franchise without militancy. The Union's suspicions of the political system proved justified: the women's suffrage amendments were ruled out of order – meaning they could not be debated – and the bill was later dropped anyway.

Emmeline and Christabel could now proclaim the constitutionalists had let them down again. Only militancy could deliver the vote. From arson the militants progressed to sabotage and bomb-making. Pillar boxes were set on fire or their contents damaged with acid – the first organised attack on the general public – and telegraph and telephone wires were cut. The orchid house at Kew Gardens and the refreshment house at Regent's Park were burned down. The turf was damaged on golf courses and acid used to cut 'Votes for Women' into greens. Emmeline commented: *Golf green activity really aroused more hostility against us than all the window-breaking.*[105] Packages addressed to Lloyd George and the Prime Minister burst into flames.

St Catherine's church, Hatcham, London torched during the WSPU arson campaign, May 1913.

As Sylvia described it: 'Women, most of them very young, toiled through the night across unfamiliar country, carrying heavy cases of petrol and paraffin. Sometimes they failed, sometimes they succeeded in setting fire to an untenanted building – all the better if it were the residence of a notability – or a church, or other place of historic interest.'[106]

In the high point of destruction of this part of the campaign, on 19 February 1913 a bomb blew up a house being built for Lloyd George in Surrey. Emmeline realised her role was not to be part of a guerrilla band of saboteurs but to encourage them on so she would be tried for sedition and stimulate publicity for the cause. *If you read your papers they say 'Clues to the perpetrators of the outrage to Mr Lloyd George's house!' A galosh! Two hatpins without heads! Two hairpins! and they are still searching, and I who have accepted responsibility several times, why have they not taken me?*[107] Emmeline was now arrested for sedition and, as she would not agree to refrain from political activity, was remanded to Holloway where Sylvia was already incarcerated and was being forcibly fed.

After two days of a hunger strike Emmeline's case was moved to the Old Bailey. This would give her the platform she required, so she agreed to conditions of bail and was released. Sylvia smuggled a letter out of prison to her mother describing her struggle against forcible feeding, which Emmeline released to the press. Sylvia also smuggled out a letter to Hardie but Emmeline withheld it from him and later, when Sylvia was released, returned the letter to her. Sylvia never forgave her mother this cruel and unpleasant act at a time when she was suffering for the cause.

The dynamic of militancy demanded that there must always be a more pressing reason, a more urgent need for the vote which would compel the audience to even greater acts of personal courage and sacrifice. Emmeline had always preached that great social

Two suffragettes in the dock at Bow Street Magistrates' Court

evils were gender-based and argued, sometimes rightly, that a range of disabilities suffered by women could be remedied only if women had the vote. By late 1912 more realistic horrors were not enough and Emmeline was turning her attention to a supposed trade in prostitutes. *Until women have the Vote, the White Slave Trade will continue all over the world . . . Even if we tolerated the degradation of the grown woman, can we tolerate the degradation of the helpless little children?* she asked, parading for her audiences stories of pregnant girls and syphilitic children, evils to be eradicated by the franchise along with prostitution.[108] Those with a grasp of politics as it is practised found Emmeline's approach absurdly simplistic. There were undoubtedly terrible sexual crimes and it was undoubtedly just for women to have the vote, but the connection between these two existed largely in the mind of Emmeline and her eager listeners.

She used the same argument at her trial at the Old Bailey for inciting others to cause explosions: *Only this morning I have had information brought to me which could be supported by sworn affidavits, that there is in this country, in this very city of London of ours, a regulated traffic, not only in women of full age, but in little children . . . well these are the things that have made us determined to go on.* She also told an anecdote about a judge found dead in a brothel on the morning of a day on which he was to try a case, which did not go down particularly well with her own trial judge.[109] The jury was sufficiently unimpressed to find her guilty, but they did make a strong recommendation to mercy. The judge felt that given the seriousness of the crime, the minimum sentence he could give was three years' penal servitude.

The day after sentencing a new explosion of militancy signalled the WSPU's defiance. Annie Kenney urged everyone to do one militant deed in the next two days. More bombing and arson followed with a new development: the smashing of the glass protecting famous paintings. Sylvia, an artist herself, was

The house of Liberal MP and industrialist Arthur du Cros at St Leonards, Hastings, burnt down on 14 April 1913

particularly disturbed by this attack on 'the spiritual offspring of the race'.[110] In the week following Emmeline's sentencing there were arson attacks on five houses at Hampstead Garden Suburb, one at Potters Bar and two mansions at Chorleywood and Norwich. Oxted station was bombed and a carriage wrecked by a bomb at Stockport. Sporting venues were also targeted with successful attacks on Ayr racecourse stand and at Duthie Park, Aberdeen where 'Release Mrs Pankhurst' was cut into the turf in huge letters.

MILITANCY THROUGHOUT THE COUNTRY

Empty House Burnt Down. Damage £1,800. No Arrests

DISCOVERY OF A SUFFRAGETTES' ARSENAL

Colliery Barges Scuttled

EXTENSIVE RAIDS ON PILLAR-BOXES

Protests at Liberal Ministers' Meetings

LABOUR MEMBERS HECKLED

Headlines at the top of a single page of *The Suffragette*, 21 March 1913

Supporters kept a vigil outside the gates of Holloway where Emmeline went on a hunger strike that lasted nine days. She tried to keep her spirits up by singing suffragette songs but felt the end was near and wrote a farewell message to Ethel Smyth including the words: *I want you to know how happy I am, lifted above these dismal surroundings and feel certain that if I am to die good will come of my going.*[111]

The Home Secretary Reginald McKenna and his officials had been pondering the problem of suffragette militancy. When arrested for criminal acts suffragettes went on hunger strike. Many people, including many MPs, felt they should be allowed to die but McKenna disagreed, fearing the creation of suffragette martyrs. Protests over the 'torture' of forcible feeding had made the procedure counter-productive: it restored the sympathy for the women's cause that they had forfeited by their acts of vandalism. The Home Office therefore rushed through a measure to release prisoners

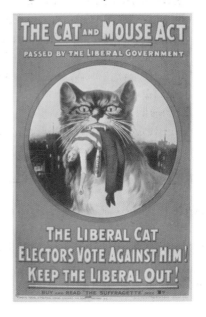

until they had recovered sufficiently to be re-imprisoned to complete the sentence. It became notorious as the 'Cat and Mouse Act', a name given it by Frederick Pethick Lawrence, who was still editing *Votes for Women*.

Emmeline received a visit from the prison governor, who read out the licence saying she was released for fifteen days provided she inform the police of all her movements. True to form, when presented with the licence as she was released, she summoned her remaining strength to tear it up, saying she had no intention of keeping to it. There was little the prison officers could do: they needed to release her. No doubt no one genuinely believed in the conditions. She went to 9 Pembridge Gardens, the nursing home run by Catherine Pine where many hunger strikers were nursed back to health. *O kind fate that has cast me for this glorious role in the history of woman!* she wrote to Ethel Smyth.[112]

Emmeline had lost a stone. She was too weak to walk and too ill to digest solid food so was fed on raw egg and lemon. While she was out, detectives attempted to keep her under observation. During one release when she was staying at Ethel's home, two detectives were watching the house, getting scant protection from the rain from gorse bushes. Ethel wished to send them umbrellas but Emmeline insisted: *Nothing of the sort. Don't make things pleasant for them!* The men would plead when they arrested her that they were only doing their duty. '*More shame on you for doing it then*, she would reply, and out shot one of the fierce flashes those soft eyes could emit when they chose.[113]

As Emmeline recovered she realised she had to keep up the momentum of protest and imprisonment. Staying with friends under the eyes of the police was not the behaviour of a leader. Accordingly, she gave notice that she would attend a WSPU rally, was stopped by detectives and re-arrested. She had already prepared a defiant address for someone to deliver in her stead at the meeting.

Suffragettes engaged in window-breakings, formerly objects of sympathy or curiosity, now had to be protected by police from hostile crowds. The suffragettes were working dangerously close to the point where they alienated more people with their crimes than the government propelled towards the cause by its persecution of them. The Union needed to take the movement to a new level if it was to maintain the edge: they had to do what the government was resisting and create a martyr. Emmeline had thought it would be her; in fact it was to be Emily Wilding Davison.

Hunger and Thirst Strike: 1913–1914

Emily Wilding Davison was a freelance revolutionary with a flair for putting herself into the action. She had first come into prominence in 1909 when she had resisted forcible feeding in Manchester prison by barricading herself in her cell, and the authorities had used a powerful fire hose to prise her out. During a protest over the census in 1911 she had hidden herself in a broom cupboard in the House of Commons overnight so she could give that address as her place of residence. She was, as has been mentioned, the first to commit arson in the name of suffrage.

Tall, slender, with green eyes and red hair, the daughter of a shopkeeper in Morpeth, Northumberland, Davison had gained a first-class degree and worked as a teacher until her activity for the WSPU with its repeated imprisonments made regular employment impossible. She was never on the Union payroll, however, or part of its leadership. 'Far from the inner circle of the Union', as Sylvia tactfully put it, she was deliberately excluded as being too extreme even for Emmeline and her coterie.[114] It was actually Davison, with unnamed

THE LATE MISS E.W. DAVISON.

Memorial picture of Emily Wilding Davidson

colleagues, who destroyed Lloyd George's house in the Union's first major bomb attack.

She wrote as early as the fire hose incident of her readiness for martyrdom. Twice she threw herself over railings in Holloway where she was caught by wire netting placed there to prevent suicide attempts and then threw herself further down, sustaining injuries on the iron staircase below. 'The idea in my mind,' she wrote, 'was that some desperate protest must be made to put a stop to the hideous torture, and one great tragedy might save others.'[115]

She was still suffering from her injuries when she attended a WSPU bazaar on 3 June 1913 and laid a wreath on a statue of Joan of Arc. The following day she went alone to Epsom, reached a place near the front of the track and as the Derby horses neared, slipped under the rail and threw herself at the King's horse. She was thrown to the ground and trampled; her skull was fractured and she did not recover.

Emmeline had been so ill that she had been released from her re-incarceration after a few days on a seven-day licence. It was generally believed in the movement that Emmeline's death would take place soon; she feared that this had been weighing on Davison's mind. Emmeline wrote in *The Suffragette* that *Our brave comrade . . . has given her life to call attention to the intolerable grievances of women. We who remain to carry on the Holy War for the emancipation of our sex dedicate ourselves anew to service and sacrifice.*[116] In deep mourning she stepped out of a flat she had been loaned in Westminster on 14 June 1913 to go to the funeral and was re-arrested by four detectives and taken to Holloway. This was a characteristically unwise move of the authorities: in place of Emmeline her carriage was driven empty behind the coffin, emphasising the leader's closeness to death. A standard-bearer with a huge wooden cross led the procession. Thousands of women in white carried lilies while others in

The funeral cortège for Emily Davidson passing through London

purple and black carried purple irises and crimson peonies. Vast crowds watched, mostly in reverence.

Davison's martyrdom played to a 19th-century ideal only destroyed in World War One, that sacrifice has meaning and everything works out for the best in a historical pageant of progress bought by suffering. The *Daily Herald*, for example, remarked on the funeral: 'we are all battling in the faith that nothing in the struggle and sacrifice is in vain, and that the end will be harmony and joyance.'[117] 'O deed majestic! O triumphant death!' wrote Sylvia in a threnody she sent to the *Daily Mail*.[118]

Several commentators certainly remarked how the suffragettes were regarded with more seriousness now it was appreciated that they were prepared to die for the cause. Christabel expressed it thus: 'Emily Davison paid with her life for making the whole world understand that women were in earnest for the vote.'[119] Emmeline went immediately on hunger strike and was released in two days; the authorities did not want another martyr. She was re-arrested nine times between May 1913 and July 1914.

Once again Emmeline pushed the government to the limits of absurd brutality by making it act out the provisions of the Cat and Mouse Act with a food-and-water strike and by deliberately exhausting herself. She described her tactics to Ethel Smyth: *I said to the Doctor 'Two nights I have lain there (pointing to the floor). From now on I will not do that but shall walk the floor until I am let go or die.'* She kept this up until he told her she would be released and said, '*You have achieved your end and I suppose you think me a tool of the government.*' Emmeline commented: *I felt it was a battle of wills. Well, mine was the strongest.*[120] When released she would often travel to France to see Christabel, the Home Secretary taking the sensible decision that he could not stop her. This was doubtless on the same logic that led him to leave Christabel abroad unmolested: she was far less trouble out of the country and it would be foolish to attempt to extradite a person for political offences.

Hunger striking reduces a prisoner's weight very quickly, but thirst striking reduces weight so alarmingly fast that prison doctors were at first thrown into absolute panic of fright . . . I am not sure that I can convey to the reader the effect of days spent without a single drop of water taken into the system. The body cannot endure loss of moisture. It cries out in protest with every nerve. The muscles waste, the skin becomes shrunken and flabby, the facial appearance alters horribly, all these outward symptoms being eloquent of the acute suffering of the entire physical being. Every natural function is, of course, suspended, and the poisons which are unable to pass out of the body are retained and absorbed. The body becomes cold and shivery, there is constant headache and nausea, and sometimes there is fever. The mouth and tongue become coated and swollen, the throat thickens and the voice sinks to a thready whisper.

Emmeline Pankhurst,
My Own Story

Margaret Holmes, later Lady Stansgate, may be taken as typical of contemporary attitudes to the suffragettes among politically aware women. She always insisted that she and her mother were 'suffragists not suffragettes'. 'We were fervent supporters of women's suffrage and were members of Millicent Fawcett's National Union of Women's Suffrage Societies, the suffragists. Being opposed to violence, we did not support the Women's Social and Political Union, the suffragettes, although we went to meetings addressed by the Pankhursts and were horrified by the forcible feeding inflicted on Mrs Pankhurst and others in prison.' So for this impressionable young Liberal, WSPU violence was a negative, the Pankhursts' speaking ability was in their favour, and forcible feeding generated sympathy and horror. In fact, though often on hunger strike, Emmeline was never forcibly fed, but she was so closely associated with the movement that she was thought of as the typical hunger-strike victim.[121]

The chaotic organisation of the WSPU deteriorated with the loss of its leaders to exile, imprisonment or expulsion. An already difficult situation had been exacerbated by the arrest and imprisonment on 30 April 1913 of many of the WSPU headquarters' staff and a chemist who were later accused of conspiracy to damage property. One of the less able organisers, Grace Roe, eluded the police and continued to operate as chief organiser in London. She rose to the occasion. The police had seized copy for an edition of *The Suffragette* but Roe organised the writing, printing and distribution of an alternative edition, to Emmeline's delight. The printers of *The Suffragette* were then prosecuted for printing material that was an incitement to arson. Open-air suffragette meetings had been banned in April, which was of course an incitement not only to suffragettes but radicals, socialists and anyone else who resisted the state's control over the right of assembly.

Annie Kenney, another released 'mouse', was in a similar situation to Emmeline: a closely guarded invalid who, as soon as she had sufficient strength, had to be whisked off to attend a speaking engagement using disguise and subterfuge. Emmeline attended a meeting to commemorate her 55th birthday on 14 July 1913 to give the defiant call *I mean to be a voter in the land that gave me birth or they shall kill me, and my challenge to the government is: Kill me or give me my freedom: I shall force you to make that choice.*[122] Annie Kenney had also spoken and was rushed by police as she left, to be defended by her supporters. Emmeline managed to escape in the mêlée. Five days later, despite the intervention of her supporters and bystanders, the police succeeded in arresting Emmeline outside Westminster Mansions. Only later did they discover that they had taken away a decoy: Emmeline had slipped out into a car that had been waiting in a side street.

Emmeline wrote to Ethel Smyth: *As for our fighting women they are in great form and very proud of their exploits as you can imagine. The girl who had her head cut open would not have it stitched as she wanted to keep the scar as big as possible! The real warrior spirit!* Accounts of Emmeline's various escapes were printed in *The Suffragette* and found their way into the newspapers where they 'could not but appeal to a sporting race like the English'.[123]

'Save Emmeline Pankhurst!
Spare her! Save her!
Give her light and set her free.
Save her! Save her!
Hear us while we pray to thee.'
Words chanted by suffragettes to interrupt church services

Emmeline stayed as the guest of one well-wisher after another as she publicly dodged the police and attended meetings in various states of frailty. Leading personalities argued for her to be pardoned. The Cat and Mouse Act was not only exciting public indignation, it was bringing the law into disrepute. The resumption of forcible feeding in December 1913, which of course the Cat and Mouse Act was intended to obviate, added to the government's difficulty in dealing with the suffragettes without producing any solution.

The end of 1913, when Emmeline went on another tour of North America, saw the government and WSPU in a stand-off. At the same time Emmeline and Christabel brought two trends in their thinking to fruition, neither of them in any way likely to improve the Union's fortunes: they decided to expel Sylvia and they became preoccupied with 'social purity'.

Expelling Sylvia, Exiling Adela

The repressive measures which the suffragettes had provoked the government into adopting led to major protests: George Lansbury and Sylvia had both been arrested for disobeying restrictions on meetings. Keir Hardie and Sylvia, among other such leading lights as the trade unionist Ben Tillett and feminist Charlotte Despard, addressed a large demonstration in Trafalgar Square supported by socialists and feminists.

Emmeline did not attend. She and Christabel were concerned that Sylvia was too close to the Labour party, which they were denouncing for its support for the Liberal government. Ironically, the non-militant National Union of Women's Suffrage Societies was now supporting Labour, which had agreed to support women's suffrage and to vote against any franchise bill that did not include women: all that Emmeline had ever asked of it.

The WSPU's anti-Labour policy made Keir Hardie a target of *The Suffragette*. Sylvia told him to keep his distance from her as 'it was too painful, too incongruous he should come in the midst of the warfare waged against him and the Labour party by orders of my sister.' He came to her during one of her Cat and Mouse releases, while she was convalescing after a hunger strike. The following day, she later wrote, describing her mother formally, as she usually did: 'It was Mrs Pankhurst who came to my bedside . . . She complained that she had intended to visit me the previous day, but learnt that Keir Hardie was coming and feared to encounter him. She spoke as if he were a person a suffragette should be ashamed to meet.'[124] Sylvia remarks that this showed how their difference of opinion on tactics had destroyed Emmeline's friendship with Hardie but it seems obvious that to meet her daughter's lover over Sylvia's prostrate body, as she had done after an earlier hunger strike, was too much for Emmeline. The 31-year-old Sylvia 'answered her reproaches with sadness: "He will not come again"'.[125]

Sylvia's relationship with Hardie was an open secret among Emmeline's close companions. Ethel Smyth, much more sensitive than Emmeline to the way in which emotional and political life are entwined, wrote to Emmeline: 'Sylvia will never be an Amazon. If it isn't J K[eir] H[ardie] it will be someone else.'[126] Sylvia had followed a widely divergent path from that laid down by Christabel. She had stayed in East London and had developed her East London Federation of the WSPU. With the fragmentation of the national leadership, this developed in time into a virtually autonomous body with its own militia – a 'citizen's army' that protected Sylvia from the police – its own wealthy funders devoted to Sylvia and, most disturbingly for Emmeline and Christabel, its own policy of co-operating with men.

Sylvia had a close political relationship with George Lansbury and with the Men's Federation for Women's Suffrage and had been urging Lloyd George to promote an adult suffrage bill, against WSPU policy. She went too far by speaking to a huge

An idealised figure of Justice on the cover of Christabel's newspaper trade union and socialist meeting in the Albert Hall in November 1913 in the company of men including George Lansbury, James Connolly and Frederick Pethick Lawrence. Christabel affirmed in *The Suffragette* that Sylvia had attended in a personal capacity and not as a speaker from the WSPU. Sylvia countered by sending a circular to local Union branches to say that in speaking at the Albert Hall she had addressed a 10,000-strong audience about women's suffrage; the Union was not holding such meetings itself any more and had not been asking her to speak in spite of its shortage of speakers.

With Emmeline in prison, evading arrest or abroad and Christabel in exile, the errant Sylvia was free to run her socialist offshoot of the WSPU as she wished. It was the potential involvement of Adela that seemed to stimulate the final confrontation between Emmeline and Christabel on one side and Sylvia and Adela on the other.

Emmeline had been away in North America for the last months of 1913, receiving none too warm a reception from American suffragists. They had made great progress by peaceful means – ten states had already given women the vote – and felt they did not need exhortations to Pankhurst-style militancy. Back in England Emmeline was arrested before she could disembark from her boat, again imprisoned, went on hunger strike, and was released twice before the end of the year. This allowed her to visit Christabel for Christmas and discuss how to reassert control over the movement – by disciplining family members.

Adela had taken work on a farm after finishing her horticultural course but she gave up, finding it excessively arduous and that it had not offered her the opportunities that she had hoped for. Once more aimless, Adela was offered a position by Sylvia in the East End, where she could use her left-wing sister's seasoned talents as a political organiser. Adela in fact refused, unwilling to break her promise not to speak in public again.

She was terrified of the reaction of her mother and Christabel and did not want to join Sylvia's camp against them. Emmeline and Christabel did not know this, however, and Christabel in particular feared the creation of a strong alternative Pankhurst faction under Sylvia's able leadership. Both women had to be summoned to Paris, one after the other, to receive their orders to quit the movement.

Early in 1914, Sylvia, weak and tired from hunger strikes and forcible feeding, was able to evade arrest and slip out of the country via Harwich and Holland. At the Paris meeting Emmeline, also unwell, was 'blanched and emaciated', leaving Christabel easily the strongest of the trio. She said they wanted to expel the East London Federation. Pressed for the reason Christabel said it was because Sylvia had spoken at the Albert Hall meeting. 'You have a democratic constitution for your Federation,' she went on, 'we do not agree with that.' The Federation put the weakest and least educated women in the fore-front by representing working women. 'We want picked women, the very strongest and most intelligent.'[127] Sylvia felt Emmeline would have been prepared to accept a compromise but Christabel insisted on a complete separation of her organisation from theirs. So it was agreed.

Sylvia returned to London to develop her autonomous Federation. Shortly after this Emmeline came to see Sylvia in the East End. They had a bad-tempered exchange over the Federation's choice of name: the East London Federation of the Suffragettes. Emmeline did not want Sylvia to use the word 'suffragettes', as she claimed it exclusively. Sylvia said her membership had chosen the name, not her, and she would not interfere. Emmeline showed how family antagonism spilled over into policy matters in an emotional letter about the organisation's name where she wrote: *You are unreasonable always have been and I fear always will be. I suppose you were made so!*[128]

> The Fathers of the old Church made a mess of the world by teaching the Adam story and classing women as unclean; the Mothers of the new Church are threatening the future by the whitewashing of women and the doctrine of the uncleanness of men.
>
> Teresa Billington-Greig, *The Truth About White Slavery*

Having expelled Sylvia, Emmeline and Christabel summoned Adela. Emmeline's youngest daughter was a curious mixture of courage and timidity. She was an extremely good platform speaker and was to make a name for herself in the rough-and-tumble of working-class politics. Yet faced with her mother's dismissal, her eloquence deserted her and she acted like a frightened animal. Emmeline decided Adela must go and start a new life in Australia, which made her feel even more unloved and miserable, but she went off as instructed. Emmeline gave her the one-way fare, some warm clothes and £20. Emmeline would never see her again.

The main reason for the split with Sylvia was clearly political, but Sylvia's active sex life (though her physical relationship with Hardie was over by 1914) must also have troubled her mother and sister. For her part, Sylvia found Christabel's new-found interest in sex both curious and revolting: 'She who had depre- cated and shunned every mention of her sex, now hinged the greater part of her propaganda upon the supposed greater preva- lence of venereal disease and the sex excesses of men.'[129]

Since April 1913 Christabel had been writing in *The Suffragette* about venereal diseases and 'white slavery' – a supposed racket in which large numbers of British innocents were trafficked, coerced into brothels abroad and held there against their will. Teresa Billington-Greig comprehensively demolished this unlikely scenario in print after detailed investigations in seven cities established that in the whole of 1912 only one girl reported as missing was recorded to have been abducted, and males were far more likely to go missing than females; but those in the grip of a moral panic are not prone to being troubled by the facts.

She excoriated 'the Pankhurst domination', arguing that 'it set women on the rampage against evils they knew nothing of, for remedies they knew nothing about. It fed on flattery the silly notion of the perfection of woman and the dangerous fellow notion of the indescribable imperfection of man.'[130]

Women voters go to the polls in Cheyenne, Wyoming, USA. 1888

On her American tour of 1913 Emmeline sold copies of *The Suffragette* and was able to promote women's suffrage as a cure for such ills as the 70 to 80 per cent of men who Christabel claimed had venereal disease before marrying innocent women. This focus on the lively subject of sex was a gift for Emmeline. Her militant policy was not popular in the US and, though she did not repudiate the policy, it was wise to concentrate on other aspects of the movement. Sometimes she combined both as she explained for a New York audience: *A broken window is a small thing when one considers the broken lives of women, and it is better to burn a house than to injure little children. This is a holy war.*[131]

The sexual diseases are the great cause of physical, mental and moral degeneracy, and of race suicide. As they are very widespread (from 70 to 80 per cent of men being infected with gonorrhoea, and a considerable percentage, difficult to ascertain precisely, being infected with syphilis), the problem is one of appalling magnitude . . . The cure, briefly stated, is Votes for Women and Chastity for Men . . . Drugs and medical concoctions will not wash away the mental and moral injury sustained by the men who practise immorality, nor are they adequate as a cure for the body . . . Regulation of vice and enforced medical inspection of the White Slaves is equally futile, and gives a false appearance of security which is fatal. Chastity for men – or, in other words, their observance of the same moral standard as is observed by women – is therefore indispensable.

Christabel Pankhurst, *The Great Scourge and How to End It*

Sexually-transmitted diseases were indeed a great curse, but Emmeline and Christabel's view was backward-looking, applying the 'moral purity' rhetoric of the late 19th century in increasingly exaggerated terms. Progressive doctors and social reformers in the first decades of the 20th century were moving from guilt-centred anti-VD programmes stressing abstinence towards social hygiene programmes that stressed treatment and prevention by barrier methods.

In Emmeline's interpretation sex was an imposition of men on women rather than a consenting activity. By blurring the boundaries between consenting and abusive sexual acts Emmeline tended to hold the sex act itself in suspicion, to demean sexually active women, and to portray women as victims of marauding men rather than active sexual beings in their own right. A new magazine which emerged at this time, *The Freewoman*, edited by Dora Marsden, a former paid organiser for the WSPU, offered a far more 20th-century view of sexual freedom for women.

The idea that enfranchised women would promote regressive sexual legislation in preference to any other kind of legislation played into the hands of the opponents of women's suffrage, who could claim that 'on sex matters women were narrower and harder than men; and that if they were given power they would impose impossibly strict standards of morality, and endeavour to enforce them by penalties for non-observance'.[132] Emmeline did nothing to allay these fears.

On the same social purity note, Christabel had a collection of her *Suffragette* essays published as *The Great Scourge and How to*

End It, warning women against venereal disease and its impact on marriage under the slogan 'Votes for Women and Chastity for Men'. The bold words and deeds of the WSPU had been reduced to absurd sloganeering.

Mouse on the Run

Christabel's long absence was a strategic mistake. She was too distanced from thinking in Britain and was open to criticism that while women were suffering to carry on militant work, she was living in idleness and some comfort in a Paris apartment and in the homes of wealthy continental supporters.

Emmeline always argued that protecting Christabel from suffering and imprisonment made it possible for her to lead the WSPU. Christabel would also be free and strong to carry on the fight when Emmeline died. Christabel was criticised for being prepared to sacrifice Emmeline to the struggle, but the sacrifice was profoundly Emmeline's own. After one release she wrote jauntily to Ethel: *There has been less waste of tissue than on previous occasions and the blood poisoning was not quite so bad either.*[133]

Death was imminent for Emmeline, with her repeated hunger and thirst strikes and the buffeting she received in each re-arrest, particularly as she now always tried to evade arrest and had a bodyguard of strong women with India-rubber clubs to keep the police at bay while she made good her escape. Most of the other hunger strikers were healthy women in their 20s and 30s. Emmeline was a middle-aged woman, who had had five children and had never been in particularly robust health, having always suffered from gastric problems. In any reasonable expectation, either women would get the vote or Emmeline would die trying to attain it. An important part of Emmeline's quality as a leader was her willingness to lead from the front.

She was not only unafraid to die, but prepared to embrace death as a furtherance of the cause.

Prior to Emmeline's speaking engagements her whereabouts were a mystery to all but a chosen few. When she was due to speak in Glasgow in March 1914 the 'Bodyguard' were summoned to go up by night train, where they travelled disguised as a touring theatrical group, sleeping using their India-rubber truncheons as pillows. The meeting, widely advertised as featuring Emmeline, had been arranged at St Andrew's Hall. On the assumption that the police would rush the platform, the organisers placed barbed-wire entanglements in front of it, disguised by garlands of flowers and leaves and tissue paper in Union colours. The Bodyguard stood as a military force across the back of the platform. Two hours before the meeting was due to start, 50 policemen occupied the basement of the building. A cordon of police surrounded it and plain-clothes detectives scrutinised each member of the crowd as they entered for a meeting due to begin at 8pm. The audience was becoming restive when the meeting did not start on time but at 8.15pm a frail, white-haired woman dressed in grey velvet presented her ticket as a member of the public and walked in, as many other elderly women did, in most cases more from curiosity than a passionate advocacy of the WSPU. It was, of course, Emmeline, who walked around the gallery and down onto the well-defended platform to wild applause and shouts of welcome. She began to speak, without notes and with no further preamble: *Today in the House of Commons has been witnessed the triumph of militancy – men's militancy – and tonight I hope to make it clear to the people in this meeting that if there is any distinction to be drawn at all between militancy in Ulster and the militancy of women it is all to the advantage of the women.*[134]

The sound of heavy boots announced an invasion. The police burst through the doors and stormed the stage where the Bodyguard were waiting. Emmeline disappeared amid a throng of flailing arms as the police laid about them with truncheons and the Bodyguard met them wielding their clubs. To add to the confusion, the audience started to join in, angered at the police disruption of a perfectly lawful meeting, and in defence of the speaker they had just welcomed. Elderly ladies in boxes near the stage laid about the heads of policemen trying to climb onto the platform; the table was overturned and chairs strewn about as the police beat the Bodyguards out of the way and seized Emmeline. Her clothes were torn, her bag and fountain pen snatched from her and the chain around her neck was ripped off as she was dragged through the crowd, her ankles and legs being badly kicked.

She was pushed into a cab filled with detectives and a police matron where she was thrown on the floor. She asked to be allowed to sit down but was told she was 'a bad woman' by one officer and struck on the back. Another opined that there would 'be a murder soon.'[135] Emmeline immediately went on a hunger and thirst strike and was released in five days.

This was an unpleasant beating for Emmeline, but the most significant aspect of it was the use by one suffragette, Janie Allen, of a pistol, which she stood and fired directly at a policeman. She had loaded it with blanks, but the threat was perfectly clear: next time it might be loaded.

It is in the context of this violence that such actions as the destruction of the Rokeby Venus should be seen. Suffragettes had slashed paintings in galleries before but Mary Richardson, a 31-year-old journalist who had also been involved in arson, took this form of militancy to a new level. She entered the National Gallery with a foot-long meat-cleaver on 10 March 1914 and repeatedly slashed the painting, a Velázquez masterpiece and one of the nation's prime art treasures. On arrest she declared: 'Yes, I am a suffragette. You can get another picture but you cannot get a life and they are killing Mrs Pankhurst.' A statement was later issued: 'I have tried to destroy the picture of the most beautiful woman

Mary Richardson under arrest for slashing a Velázquez masterpiece at the National Gallery

in mythological history as a protest against the government for destroying Mrs Pankhurst, who is the most beautiful character in modern history. Justice is an element of beauty as much as colour and outline on canvas. Mrs Pankhurst seeks to procure justice for womanhood, and for this she is being slowly murdered by a government of Iscariot politicians.'[136] Militancy had now advanced so far from its object that it seemed mere vandalism. It became world news but only because of its bizarre and terrible nature. It was not a good advertisement for women's suffrage.

The destruction escalated for the first seven months of 1914. Sylvia records that three great houses in Scotland were damaged by fire on a single night; the Carnegie Library in Birmingham suffered an arson attack; more pictures were slashed; ancient churches were blown up. There were 141 acts of destruction reported in the press and 107 cases of arson.[137] *The public were thrown into a state of emotion of insecurity and frightened expectancy,*

Emmeline declared, while frankly acknowledging that: *Not yet did they show themselves ready to demand of the government that the outrages be stopped in the only way they could be stopped – by giving votes to women.*[138]

Suffragettes were more defiant but less popular. Those with no taste for destruction or acts that would incur prison sentences took to interrupting services at churches, theatre performances and meals at restaurants. It seemed an increasingly desperate development that played into the hands of those who would describe suffragettes as hysterical. Though militant acts of all kinds helped to keep women's suffrage on the agenda, they brought no improvement in the political scene.

For man the physiology and psychology of woman is full of difficulties . . . no doctor can ever lose sight of the fact that the mind of woman is always threatened with danger from the reverberations of her physiological emergencies. It is with such thoughts that the doctor lets his eyes rest on the militant suffragist. He cannot shut them to the fact that there is mixed up with the women's movement much mental disorder; and he cannot conceal from himself the physiological emergencies that lie behind.

The recruiting field for the militant suffragists is the half million of our excess female population – that half million which had better long ago have gone out to mate with its complement of men beyond the seas.

Sir Almorth Wright, *The Times*, 28 March 1912

The campaign reached a high pitch with an escalation of the Irish crisis. The Ulster Unionists armed themselves and began drills to demonstrate their intention to fight for an independent state. This strategy was both persuasive to the government and an indication to the suffragettes that more militancy could be successful where less had failed. Emmeline decided she must address women's suffrage as a constitutional issue, like that of Ireland, and approach the King directly, as the Ulster protesters had, bypassing a recalcitrant Parliament.

Months of preparation went into the march on Buckingham Palace, to *carry our demand for justice to the throne of the Monarch.*[139] While attention-grabbing, the idea that an appeal to the King was likely to have practical results was a demonstration of how far Emmeline had moved into the Conservative camp, where the monarchy was seen as a guardian of decency and fair play. For those with whom Richard and Emmeline Pankhurst had once mixed, the monarch was merely a bastion of class privilege.

She used the same technique she had used to rush Parliament: she asked for an audience with the King and when it was refused called for a march on Buckingham Palace on 21 May 1914. To this end, a large house in Grosvenor Place overlooking Buckingham Palace was borrowed by the WSPU from a sympa-

The Suffragettes storm Buckingham Palace, 21 May 1914

thiser and unostentatiously filled with WSPU members from three days before the date of the demonstration until there were 200 staying there, including Emmeline. All were given a piece of paper with the address of a sympathiser which they must memorise as their place of escape if they were not arrested; then the papers were burned. Newspapers had reported that the women would be driven back at the point of bayonets so when they set out the company of women marching ten abreast behind Emmeline could easily have been marching into far greater danger than they had seen previously.

Other women, who had been watching the march, joined the company as it marched past the back wall of the palace garden. Together they met the police at the gates of the palace, throwing eggs filled with coloured powder. Some women tried to climb the palace gates and the Bodyguard wielded their rubber clubs to clear a path for Emmeline. The police retaliated by beating the women with truncheons and throwing them to the ground. Confronted with mounted police, the suffragettes cut the bridles of the horses so their riders could not control them; in a comical gender-specific guerrilla tactic they cut the braces of policemen so they would be hampered by falling trousers.

The Bodyguard fought a way for Emmeline through the cordon, through Wellington Gate and a cordon at the bottom of Constitution Hill. She nearly reached the front of the palace when a large policeman gripped her in a bear-hug from behind and carried her off as she called out: *Arrested at the gates of the palace – tell the King!*[140] The widely published picture of Emmeline lifted off her feet but still calling out went round the world and stimulated more attacks on paintings and museum exhibits, bombs in churches and water mains.

Now well-versed in the tactics of maximum resistance, the arrested women refused to give their names and changed clothes in detention so that identification was difficult. They sang and shouted slogans when taken to court and refused to be bound over, eventually being discharged. Emmeline endured her eighth hunger and thirst strike and was discharged in seven days. She was tormented by hearing the cries of women being forcibly fed who had come to prison for carrying out her policies: *It is all very well for me; I have the limelight*, she said, *but these!*[141]

Arrested ... tell the King!

In a debate in the House of Commons on 11 June 1914, the Home Secretary discussed actions to be taken against the suffragettes amid an atmosphere hostile to militancy. There was a genuine fear of lawlessness: that outraged members of the public would attack militants and crimes would be committed not just by the militants but also against them. He appealed to the press not to give further publicity to the militants, and such papers as the *Daily Graphic* made a point of giving space to non-militant suffrage groups.

With the arrest of WSPU general secretary, Grace Roe, all the leaders were out of action or exhausted by hunger and a fugitive life. The movement was losing the daily struggle to keep interest going in an organisation that was losing its active members. Even imprisoned suffragettes were signing agreements not to undertake further militant acts. The Home Office was planning a raid on all the wealthy sponsors of the WSPU in order to seek compensation for the destruction of property, as they had managed to do against the Pethick Lawrences. The Home Office had noted the phenomenon of how increased militancy stimulated revenue for the Union: the supporters they still had were even more willing to pay towards the exploits of militants. The Union received its largest total of donations in the year to February 1914.

Even Christabel, out of touch as she was, realised their time was over and wrote what seems to be a valedictory leader in *The Suffragette* eight days after the march on Buckingham Palace: 'The Militants will rejoice when victory comes in the shape of the vote, and yet, mixed with their joy will be regret that the most glorious chapter in women's history is closed and the militant fight over – over, while so many have not yet known the exultation, the rapture of battle.'[142] The march to the Palace was the WSPU's last great demonstration, and Emmeline's last great militant act.

Saved by the War: 1914–1916

In a brilliant outflanking move, Sylvia was preparing to wrest from the government a concession that her mother and sister had failed to achieve. In true Pankhurst style, she did it by throwing herself into a bold and desperate act: her mother would not be the first to die for the cause – she would. She told Asquith: 'I will not merely hunger strike but when I am released I will continue my hunger strike at the door of the Strangers' Entrance of the House of Commons and will not take either food or water until you agree to see my deputation.'[143] Sylvia suddenly became

Sylvia, prostate, is carried by East End supporters, June 1914

the heroine of the suffragette Grand Guignol of violence and suffering. Asquith was deeply unwilling to take any responsibility for Sylvia's self-chosen martyrdom; nor did Emmeline approve of Sylvia's raising the stakes by fasting not only in but out of prison too. *Tell her I advise her when she comes out of prison to go home and let her friends take care of her*, Emmeline replied to a sympathiser who had written to her.[144]

When she was released from Holloway, Sylvia had herself carried in procession on a stretcher to the House of Commons and laid on the steps. At the intercession of Keir Hardie, Asquith did agree to see a deputation of Sylvia's East End women on 20 June. When he received them, these women gravely and patiently told him of the present hardships of their lives which could be relieved by legislation brought in by politicians who would listen to working women only if working women had the vote. It was an argument he respected, put by people who, with millions like them, were likely to vote for his party or the allied Labour party. He said he accepted the logic of their argument and declared that: 'If the change has to come, we must face it boldly and make it thoroughgoing and democratic in its basis.'[145] This has been interpreted as accepting universal suffrage, though to so slick a politician as Asquith, words had a wider variety of meanings than they had for ordinary folk.

Asquith obviously did not settle on a solution as a result of a single meeting, but it was time to either make a concession or else damage his leadership on a question he regarded with disdain. Women's suffrage was Labour party policy and Labour was now allied with the non-militant suffragists. The Conservatives were certain to make some kind of statement on limited women's franchise before the next election, and at that election a majority of Liberal members would probably insist on women's suffrage being party policy if for no other reason than because the Women's Liberal Association would demand it as a price for their practical electoral work. Asquith might still be personally opposed, but he had to bow to the inevitable. By doing so, he was able to boast in his memoirs that he had arranged the Speaker's Conference on Representation that achieved the 1918 settlement.

Giving every adult the vote was more acceptable to Asquith than any measure Emmeline and the WSPU had proposed, particularly because Asquith resented the way the suffragettes had behaved and as a patrician he did not wish to reward bad behaviour. He always regarded the suffragettes as a hysterical sideshow and relegated reference to them in his memoirs to one paragraph in a chapter titled 'Miscellanea'.

Asquith had made a mess of the issue. He should have faced political realities much earlier and legislated for some measure of women's suffrage on the best terms for the Liberal party while they had a sufficient majority to push it through. Lloyd George, who was within two years to oust Asquith, had a more canny approach than the Prime Minister. He saw Sylvia and made a firm commitment to women's suffrage – a cause he had always supported – saying he would refuse to join the next Liberal government unless it was committed to a reform bill giving votes to women on broad, general lines. Sylvia's account of this meeting is unclear because of her faulty knowledge of parliamentary procedure, but the commitment was clearly there.

Sylvia was the Pankhurst who had gone furthest in the hunger strike and was the Pankhurst with whom the leading politicians were prepared to meet. Her memoirs are, after the fashion of such literature, self-promoting, but it is nonetheless clear that she was gaining attention and apparently making progress. Emmeline now took the initiative to herself push up the stakes, announcing in a letter to *The Times* that: *tomorrow I shall openly resume my work for the enfranchisement of women and that when they have effected my re-arrest with its usual accompaniment of brutality and insult I shall resume the strike. I challenge them to apply to me the same treatment of forcible feeding that is used in the case of my friends.*[146] She walked into the WSPU headquarters at Lincoln's Inn and was duly arrested later that day.

Her treatment was worse than she had expected. While she had previously been relatively unmolested on entry, a new regulation meant every suffragette had to be strip-searched. She resisted this indignity and fought with the wardresses until they finally overcame her and then refused to put her clothes back on, lying naked on the floor of the cell, with her last effort of will defying them to observe the indignity to which they had subjected her. With the pig-headed persistence of official regimes, the prison then subjected Emmeline to a disciplinary committee for having resisted the strip-search, which sentenced her to seven days' solitary confinement, a perfectly pointless exercise as she was on hunger strike and was released the next day having lost nearly a stone in weight.

She was heartrending to look on, her skin yellow, and so tightly drawn over her face that you wondered the bone structure did not come through; her eyes deep sunken and burning, and a deep dark flush on her cheeks. With horror I then became acquainted with one physical result of hunger-striking that still haunts me. It is due, I suppose, to the body feeding on its own tissue; anyhow the strange, pervasive, sweetish odour of corruption that hangs about a room in which a hunger-striker is being nursed back to health is unlike any other smell. I often hoped that Mrs Pankhurst, the most meticulously dainty of beings, had no idea of this sinister effect of hunger-striking and I am glad to believe she hadn't, for she would have minded that more than anything else.

Ethel Smyth,
Female Pipings in Eden

Emmeline seemed to have only two possible roles: victor or martyr. She would win or die in the attempt, and in that case victory would then be gained in her name. In her darkest hour a third possibility emerged, thanks to imperial rivalry: the World War started.

Emmeline had slipped out of the country and was in St Malo when Britain declared war on Germany after the latter's invasion of neutral Belgium during the attack on France in August 1914. Emmeline had always loved France as much as she had mistrusted Germany and, despite her disagreements with the British constitution, her first feelings were patriotic. That said, she was also dedicated to the cause and saw all developments in the light of their relevance to the WSPU: a truce was a good strategy now they had come to the end of the road with militancy.

Emmeline made the first move, ordering the WSPU membership to suspend all activity until the international crisis was over. The government wished to have an armistice over the subjects that had vexed them – Irish Home Rule, Welsh disestablishment, labour disputes and suffrage – but the Home Secretary Reginald McKenna was incapable of handling any policy cleanly and efficiently. He first declared only that he would release those prisoners who would undertake not to commit further acts of militancy: a restatement of current policy. Political pressure ensured that McKenna then announced the unconditional release of all suffrage prisoners on 10 August. Both sides could now back down without losing face.

Emmeline returned to England with Christabel, who thus ended two and a half years of exile, and who wrote in *The Suffragette* that the war was 'God's vengeance upon the people who held women in subjection'.[147] Now, however, gender roles were no longer criticised as part of the means by which women were subjected. It was right and just that men should volunteer to fight. Emmeline explained to a meeting: *the war has made me feel how much there is of nobility in man, in addition to the other thing which we all deplore.*[148] She spoke in favour of Kitchener's appeal for recruits, calling on men to join up to fight on behalf of women: they were men and must do men's work. Women must attend to their own task of building up the race, and take on war work.

Those opposed to the war and the militarization of labour became traitors for Emmeline, including such socialists as Sylvia who wrote to her mother to condemn her jingoism. Emmeline wrote back that she was *ashamed to know where you and Adela stand*.[149] When Sylvia announced that she intended to attend an international peace conference in The Hague, Emmeline accused her of being misled by German propagandists. Keir Hardie's death in 1915 added to Sylvia's unhappiness. She was unable to heal the rift with her mother: Emmeline would speak of nothing but the war. For her part, Sylvia considered her mother's support for the war effort to be a 'tragic betrayal' of the principles of the suffrage movement, for Emmeline had always proclaimed that when given the vote *Women will stand for peace*.[150]

It fitted in with her rapid transformation from destructive termagant to national treasure, that late in the summer of 1914 Emmeline's memoirs were published. An American journalist supporter, Rheta Childe Dorr, had travelled across the Atlantic with Emmeline on her 1913 lecture tour and interviewed her at length for a series of biographical articles. She later fashioned the material, together with other written sources, into a book, *My Own Story*, which of course was nothing of the sort, but a ghost-written celebrity biography. Emmeline did not write any books herself: she could not be moved to write newspaper articles even when editors were offering her commissions and she badly needed the money. When she sat to write, she said, *I always feel as if I were in the dentist's chair.*[151] The errors in *My Own Story* (it even gets the number of Emmeline's children wrong) have prompted suggestions that she did not proofread it, but Dorr's shorthand was good and much of the book is reliable as direct quotation.

In 1915 *The Suffragette* was renamed *Britannia* and edited by Christabel to promote war activities such as the range of jobs which were now being done by women, though the newspaper was suppressed over its vociferous antagonism towards Asquith and the

Foreign Secretary Lord Grey for their conduct of the war. The conflict was forging new alliances. By 1915 war production was a pressing priority for the government. Trade unionists were refusing to allow women to work in munitions factories, for fear they would lower wage rates, and supplies were running low. Emmeline had been talking about women's willingness to serve the country but in this essential work women were specifically excluded.

At the suggestion of the King, Lloyd George (now Minister of Munitions) sent for Emmeline. He explained the problem as he saw it and offered her expenses for a demonstration in favour of war work, but particularly munitions work for women. The Treasury eventually paid more than £4,000 towards the costs of Emmeline and the WSPU office staff organising a 'Call to Women' demonstration with a procession through London on 17 July 1915 behind a banner saying 'We Demand the Right to Serve'. There were only about 6,000 demonstrators but 90 bands played patriotic tunes for the marchers, who marched under red, white and blue flags in place

Women doing war work as police officers

of the familiar WSPU colours. In an imitation of armed services recruitment, women were invited to sign up to war work during the demonstration. The women marched to the Ministry of Munitions where, in marked contrast to the ministerial disdain for previous suffrage demonstrations, Lloyd George met and welcomed them. As Emmeline had been ultimately responsible for blowing up his house only two years before, past injuries were certainly being buried in the service of the war effort.

Emmeline was also recruited to tour the South Wales coalfields in a campaign to urge militant workers to set aside industrial disputes and put the nation first. Emmeline was standing shoulder to shoulder with the British state in a war which many advanced thinkers considered a betrayal of internationalist aspirations. Some have accused her of reneging on the principles she shared with her husband but, as June Purvis emphasises in her biography of Emmeline, as a 'patriotic feminist' she was still challenging some of the well-established definitions of femininity and gender roles, but in a context that was no longer subversive.[152]

In the early months of 1915 Emmeline responded to a new moral panic about 'war babies', children born to unmarried women who had sex with soldiers, widely predicted in the press to be a great social problem. Emmeline decided to set up a home for 50 illegitimate female children. Having embraced the role of friend of the government, she now wanted to take up that of mother. Why she did so is open to question. She had not eagerly embraced her role as mother to her own children and she later showed the reverse of enthusiasm for her grandchild, Sylvia's son. She had no steady income and so advertised her scheme to the WSPU but, having received no great encouragement, she reduced her proposal to adopting four girls herself. Ethel Smyth was very critical of the scheme but said: 'as well try to hold up an avalanche with a child's spade as persuade Mrs Pankhurst out of any idea that had once taken root in her mind.'[153]

Emmeline found the four girls at a children's home and took them to the nursing home owned by Catherine Pine. Emmeline later rented a house and wrote revealingly: *All these years I have persuaded myself that I did not want a home of my own. But now that I can have one I am all impatience to get into it.*[154] She was later to admit that 'the question of war babies had been exaggerated' but the four adoptees were to remain a financial burden to Emmeline as others did not flock to her support.[155]

Emmeline came under fire from WSPU members for diverting funds donated for the suffrage cause towards measures such as support for the 'war babies', only sanctioned by Emmeline herself, and not presenting audited accounts for the organisation. When Mary Leigh, the first to use 'the argument of the stone', veteran of a five-year prison sentence and many forcible feedings, tried to question Emmeline at a Union meeting, the WSPU autocrat accused her of supporting the Germans.

Christabel, who continued to live abroad, applied herself to war strategy and began to argue on the same side as Lloyd George and others for a campaign in the Balkans to undermine Germany's allies Turkey and Austria. Emmeline therefore began to focus her attention on Serbia and in 1916 went to the US to raise money for humanitarian aid for Serbia and for her four adopted children. She raised enough to set up a house in Clarendon Road, Kensington, where Catherine Pine continued to look after the girls.

An election was overdue and suffrage was again a burning issue. The current franchise was based on a property and residency qualification. Many men had changed their residence by going to fight abroad and had therefore become disenfranchised. This was obviously anomalous, as was a suggestion that only men at arms should be automatically enfranchised: should those who had been ordered to stay at home for vital war work be discriminated against? But if those men on war work were to be enfranchised, why not women on war work? The war had created an awkward conundrum for legislators, which Asquith dealt with by creating a Speaker's Conference of backbench MPs from all parties to consider the issue.

The National Union of Women's Suffrage Societies called together a joint committee of all the women's suffrage societies to present the women's case to the conference. Emmeline had sworn the WSPU off campaigning for women's suffrage until after the war and so refused to join the committee. This was hardly a matter of campaigning and she could have engaged in discussions. After having been centre-stage for so long, she may have been worried that her long-held vision of the franchise for women would not prevail (as in fact it did not). Perhaps her involvement with war work had engaged her attentions so thoroughly that it had crowded out the franchise issue. For whatever reason, Emmeline Pankhurst was to make no contribution to the technicalities of the bill that finally enfranchised some women.

Votes for Men and Women: 1917–1928

Lloyd George, always more sympathetic to the women's cause than Asquith, replaced him as Prime Minister in December 1916. The Speaker's Conference reported the following year, recommending the enfranchisement of all men on a residency qualification, all soldiers and sailors, and a women's suffrage measure with a property qualification and an age limit – 30 was eventually decided.

This 'fancy franchise' was a concession to those who feared flooding the system with working-class women who might vote along class lines and produce a Liberal or Liberal–Labour landslide. There was also concern that women should not leap from having no vote to being in a majority in one move, as there were more adult women than men. Technically, the measure was the negation of the exactly equal franchise for women and men that Emmeline and the WSPU had always argued for.

It was a victory for those who favoured compromise, which in the end included even Emmeline. The representatives of all the other suffrage societies refused to have Emmeline in a deputation going to see the Prime Minister to make final remarks about the proposals, and she was therefore invited as an individual. She said she was ready to accept any measure that could be passed with as little debate as possible.

As Lloyd George said, 'the heroic patriotism of the women workers during the war had now made their claim irresistible.'[156] Even Asquith conceded the point and dramatically intervened in the debate to say that women's war service had changed his mind. Whether this was true, or was a gracious way of submitting to the inevitable, women's war work was still central to the equation.

The House of Commons passed the Bill in December 1917 by 364 votes to 23, but Emmeline had no further interest in the subject. As Jill Craigie wrote: 'After the majority of women had been enfranchised, she was never again heard to refer to the part she had played in the suffrage agitation, and those who did lost her attention.'[157] When women's organisations asked her to be a paid worker with a campaign in the mid-1920s to give women the vote at 21, on the same terms as men, she repudiated any need for this measure. She said it would be *undesirable to re-open the franchise agitation in such a world-crisis as this, especially as women have already enough voting power, if effectively employed.*[158]

The King gave his assent to the Representation of the People Act on 6 February 1918. Women over 30 who were themselves on the local government electors' list (and so were ratepayers) or were the wives of men so qualified were placed on the register of parliamentary electors. After the Act some 8 million women and 13 million men had the vote. The same year women were allowed to stand for election to the House of Commons. The House of Lords did not admit peeresses until 1958.

Emmeline was far more interested in the WSPU's 'industrial peace' campaign aimed at combating industrial strife supposedly fomented by pacifists, German sympathisers and Bolsheviks. She was given an opportunity to deal a closer blow against Bolshevism when she was invited by the British government to visit the Russian ally in June 1917 to help shore up the moderate provisional government against Lenin's Bolsheviks. The allies feared, justifiably, that the far-left would take over in Russia and make a separate peace with Germany. By the time she and her companion Jessie Kenney (Annie's sister) arrived, the situation had gone too far in the direction of disorder and the Bolsheviks were gaining the upper hand. Emmeline was well known among the politically interested, as *My Own Story* had been translated into Russian, so she did not lack for curious visitors but the conditions in Petrograd were becoming desperate. The food was of poor quality and what they had Emmeline had difficulty in digesting because of her gastric problems; social unrest even extended to a strike in the hotel where they were staying. Emmeline tried to address meetings but was hampered by a lack of the Russian language (though she could speak to the educated in French). Local activists denounced the pair as 'bourgeois women'.[159] Emmeline travelled back to London just before the revolution but returned to the subject of Russia in June 1918 when she sailed to North America to urge international intervention in Russia to bring down the Bolsheviks.

At home Emmeline had her own ideas for political progress. The WSPU was relaunched as the Women's Party on 2 November 1917 with a programme of gender equality including equal pay and equality of opportunity of employment, but also a number of more questionable proposals such as raising the age of consent and dismissing government officials who had German family ('enemy blood' as it said) or pacifist connections. The new party opposed independence for Ireland and regarded Indian independence with extreme suspicion. It was more an autocracy than a political party. Its manifesto declared: 'Now that we women have got the vote, we are going to have a Government composed of the best people . . . we are determined to get rid of class in Government, we are going to have Governments formed, without distinctions of class, without favour to any class, of the best citizens, best in their instincts, best in their training, best in their experience to control the affairs and destinies of this Empire.'[160]

A bill allowing women to stand for the House of Commons was rushed through in November 1918. Emmeline was urged to stand but with characteristically poor judgement where her eldest daughter was concerned, she insisted the honour should go to Christabel. *She is the woman of the hour and our best representative . . . I am her most ardent disciple.*[161] 'Mrs Pankhurst said that Miss Pankhurst was the founder of the movement which had resulted in the emancipation of the women of this country.' The only reason she had not won the war, as *The Times* reported with tongue in cheek, was because she had not been allowed to: 'if her ideas had been adopted by the Government in the early days of the war many valuable lives would have been spared and peace would have been concluded long ago.'[162] Candidates who supported Lloyd George's coalition government had a 'coupon' that virtually guaranteed a seat. Christabel had intended to contest the vulnerable Liberal seat of Westbury in Wiltshire and had arranged it but at the last minute changed her mind and told Lloyd George that she wanted Smethwick, a more working-class constituency in the Midlands. Lloyd George had the already approved coalition candidate stand down in her favour. Though Christabel was standing against only one, Labour, candidate, and Emmeline worked tirelessly for her daughter, she lost. Ethel Smyth thought Emmeline found it 'the bitterest disappointment of her life'.[163]

Others did not share Emmeline's enthusiasm for Christabel standing again. Emmeline had alienated many erstwhile supporters, others had drifted away and not been replaced by new ones. Even Christabel was less interested in the parliamentary process than might have been imagined: she had converted to Adventism and was preparing for the Second Coming of Christ, a cause to which she devoted the rest of her life. The Women's Party quietly died.

In thinking that women's entry into politics was to herald a new age of superior morality where class antagonism would die, Emmeline missed the point that the most important freedoms women achieved in the first decades of the new century were personal freedoms and most of the battles were individual. Many women fought for greater opportunities in a hostile workplace, usually with little help from male-dominated trade unions. Even more divorced from Emmeline's world-view, new feminists were fighting for choice in marriage partners, for sex

on their own terms, and the
right to control their own
fertility. Her 19th-century
view of sexual morality,
together with her autocratic
attitude, left her with no
point of contact with 20th-
century feminists.

Anti-Bolshevism was a
much more attractive subject
for Emmeline and she left the
shores of Britain to lecture on
this in North America, and on
'social hygiene' (venereal disease) in Canada for five years
from September 1919. Her
four adopted daughters joined
her in Canada in 1920. The

One of the last portraits of Emmeline
Pankhurst

children adored her though she was no more affectionate to them
than she had been to her first family. They remembered a very
formal upbringing characteristic of the Victorian middle class
where they would be taken from the nursery to be presented to
her only once a day.

Supporters in England wanted to ensure that the now sexage-
narian Emmeline did not have to continue earning a living and
set up a committee to raise money for Emmeline and Christabel.
Adding Christabel was a major error: whatever affection there
was for Emmeline, the idea of stumping up to keep her eldest
daughter as well, when she was more than capable of earning her
own living, was more than anyone but the most ardent Pankhurst
fans could bear. The scheme was intended to raise £10,000 but
in fact managed only £2,866. As well as being an embarrassment, this led to a rift with Ethel Smyth, who explained the

situation to Emmeline in a letter that Emmeline returned to her with a terse note. As ever, Emmeline could tolerate no criticism of Christabel.

During this time Christabel was writing books on the Second Coming and addressing huge Adventist meetings. Adela in Australia married another political activist, a widower older than her with three children, thus giving her the family she had always yearned for, to which she was to add another four children. Sylvia continued her work in the East End, strengthened her links with the Soviet Union and even travelled to Russia to meet Lenin.

Eventually tiring of the climate and the round of lecturing in Canada, Emmeline settled in Bermuda in summer 1924. Her funds were limited and she was unwilling to continue lecturing in Canada where the climate was too extreme for her, so, after a year, she took stock and decided to return to Europe. She kept her favourite of the girls, Mary, and Christabel kept another one, Betty. The other two were sent back to Britain to be adopted by other people.

She sailed for Europe in 1925 and opened a tea shop in the south of France, which had as little success as her previous business ventures. She had underestimated the severity of the winters and when the bleak November winds came, she was compelled to leave the coast. She returned to Britain to live with her sister Ada. As Emmeline's financial situation remained precarious, she later also gave Mary away, to a couple who had adopted one of the other girls.

Emmeline had previously been a member of the Liberals, the Independent Labour Party, and the Women's Party; now her renewed interest in domestic politics found expression in the Conservatives. It was 'the party she had not yet tested' according to Sylvia.[164] She received their backing and was adopted as a parliamentary candidate in the working-class district of Whitechapel in London's East End, close to Sylvia's power base. She hired small lodgings there and set about charming the electors with her characteristic energy, public warmth and charm.

As both Christabel and Emmeline damaged their electoral chances by standing for working-class constituencies when they could have had middle-class ones, more suited to the tenor of their message, it is worth pondering why they did so. It may have been that they wanted to prove to themselves as much as to the world that the Pankhurst family's principles were still as egalitarian as they had been in Richard Pankhurst's day. Alternatively, it may have merely been a further battle in the Pankhurst family war against the younger daughters' socialism, in which Sylvia was soon to deliver a blow with lasting effect.

Sylvia had a long relationship with an Italian refugee from fascism, Silvio Corio, and had for some time attempted to get pregnant, despite their not being married. Emmeline made the paranoid accusation that Sylvia had got pregnant just to embarrass her mother, the prophet of sexual responsibility. It was a painful and unpleasant attack and Emmeline did not hide her disgust, refusing to speak to Sylvia but running upstairs and locking herself in her room when Sylvia called to see her.

Sylvia had her baby on 4 December 1927 and called him Richard after her father, whose socialist principles she believed her mother had betrayed; Keir after her lover whom her mother had repudiated; and Pethick after the couple Emmeline had expelled from the Union. Richard Keir Pethick's last name was to be Pankhurst, despite Christabel's plea that Sylvia call him after his father. To make sure her mother and sister got the message, Sylvia broadcast it to everyone in an article cabled to North American newspapers and in an interview with the *News of the World* headlined 'Sylvia's Amazing Confessions'. Sylvia was not only defiant, she was sexually defiant. Ethel Smyth read the piece and said: 'This will break Em's heart.'

Sylvia had written to her mother saying a child was due but Emmeline's sister had intercepted the letter in a stupid attempt to protect Emmeline from the knowledge. Of course this meant that when she found out, just before the *News of the World* story, it was particularly hard to take. She was asked a question about her unknown grandchild at a public meeting and responded that private matters should not be discussed in public. She finished her speech but never went on a public platform again. Ethel Smyth said Emmeline 'wept all day without ceasing . . . *I shall never be able to speak in public again*' she said over and over.[165]

Doubtless exacerbated by her unhappiness, her old gastric complaint flared up and she was unable to retain food. She died on 14 June 1928 at the age of 69 in a nursing home on Wimpole Street, a month after the final passage of the bill giving women over 21 the vote on equal terms with men, and four months after the death of her adversary Herbert Asquith.

At the huge funeral attended by thousands of women, many in WSPU colours, the chief mourners were Christabel and Sylvia, who had brought her baby son, the grandchild Emmeline never saw.

Emmeline's Achievement

Emmeline was self-promoting, but the self she was advancing was intimately connected with the cause. In terms of personal rewards, there were none. Emmeline lived in poverty for a great deal of her life. Despite her love of fine clothes and comfortable surroundings, she poured her energy and what money she had into her work. Her entire estate after her death was valued at just over £86.

In a life of such sacrifice, what did she achieve? It was unfortunate that for six of the WSPU's total of 11 years of fighting for the vote the implacably opposed Asquith was Prime Minister, but there was little doubt that the change would take place. Women's suffrage was a necessary and obvious reform in which Britain took its place among other democracies, later than some but earlier than others. Looking at the history of world suffrage movements raises an unsettling question: was the degree of militancy that Pankhurst employed – far in excess of that employed by women anywhere else in the world – really necessary in Britain?

Millicent Garrett Fawcett continued to believe that patient negotiation and a continual reminder of the numbers of supporters of women's suffrage would win the day. One might expect Fawcett, who had never believed in any form of militancy, to be sceptical, but others who had actively engaged in it also came to question its value. Emmeline Pethick Lawrence, who had been imprisoned and suffered forcible feeding for militancy, did not believe that the increased militancy after 1912 strengthened the movement or brought it closer to victory. She said attacks on private property in particular 'roused a great deal of hostility which was only partly counter-balanced by the admiration felt for the heroism of Mrs Pankhurst herself and other members of the fraternity.'[166] Lloyd George was no enemy to militant action for the cause of liberty and had himself advised it in some circumstances, but he believed the suffragette militant action had been counter-productive in parliamentary terms. It had 'transformed indifference into hostility'.[167]

The single most important cause of the enfranchisement of women was not battles on the streets but the cumulative pressure of the many battles in women's lives, in their families, where they struggled to redefine the role of daughter and wife, and in the labour market, where a vanguard demanded the right to have professional qualifications and then the right to use them. An army of women fought for the right to be employed on the same terms as men (though this was not to become national policy until the Equal Pay Act of 1970). The major legislative advances in women's rights over their own property in marriage and the right to higher education and a position in the professions, had already largely been made in the 19th century. Winning the vote was a consolidation of these 19th-century battles, public and private, fought against tradition in the deeply conservative country of Britain.

The women's suffrage movement rode the tide of democratic progress sweeping across the world. Already, by the time the WSPU was formed, women had been enfranchised in New Zealand, Australia and some states of the US. The passing years were to see them progressively joining participatory democracy in other countries.

New nations showed more willingness to enfranchise women than the European countries from which their settler populations came. In the western United States the Territory of Wyoming gave women the vote on the same basis as men in 1869. When Wyoming became a state of the Union in 1890 women's voting rights remained, blazing a trail for three further western states to enfranchise women in the 1890s. In the same decade, Western Australia and South Australia enfranchised women. The first nation in which women were able to vote on the same basis as men was New Zealand, in 1893. Five European nations gave women the vote in the 20th century before it was achieved in Britain: Finland, Norway, Iceland, Denmark and the Soviet Union. In the Netherlands women were allowed to stand for parliament in 1917 but did not have the vote until 1919. In contrast, France and Italy gave women the vote only after the Second World War.

Yet it remains the case that Britain has tended to delay the most obviously necessary reforms long past the point where they should have been enacted. Social progress has often come only with upheaval, whether riot or industrial unrest: the Brixton riots of 1981 and the Poll Tax riot of 1990 showed the continuing ability of violent uprisings to force the political agenda. In 1909 Emmeline recalled that she had joined the executive committee of the North of England Society for Women's Suffrage 29 years earlier: her experience of the first 25 years of 'constitutional methods' had taught her that only militancy would be effective.[168] Suffragettes repeatedly looked to the agitations that had achieved suffrage extensions for men in 1832, 1867 and 1884 and focused on violent incidents. Cabinet members like Gladstone and Hobhouse reinforced the view that only a masculine-style show of force would convince the government that reform was imperative.

The unanswerable case patiently made by the NUWSS might have remained unanswered until after World War Two (when nine European countries finally gave women the vote). As it was, other pressures for legislative change of the franchise caused by war and the need to update voting lists in 1918 came after Emmeline's militant methods had fixed Votes for Women as an inescapable item on the political agenda where it had previously drifted for decades.

The war work that Emmeline promoted had shown women's value and capability outside the home. By the end of the war around a million women were in jobs previously done by men. The sheer numbers involved demonstrated that all women deserved the vote, not just a superior few. Emmeline had also encouraged women to show, through their actions in the political sphere and in the world of 'men's' work, that they were fully equipped to enjoy national political rights. The popular conception that Emmeline Pankhurst was primarily responsible for obtaining the vote for at least some women in 1918, rather than later, is, on balance, justified.

The WSPU's original contribution to the practice of politics, seen at a distance of nearly a century, is more questionable. Disrupting meetings, breaking windows, marching on the House of Commons and arson fit into a tradition of riot for political ends stretching at least from the early 18th century through to such events as the anti-globalisation protests. They were not exclusively WSPU activities. Suffragette-style mass hunger striking was used to some effect by Irish Republican prisoners in the early 1980s but hunger striking has generally been a matter of individual protest. The destruction of works of art as an idealistic gesture did not catch on; like spitting at policemen, it was a suffragette dead end. A willingness to commit suicide for the cause in a dramatic gesture is even less admirable to the general public, if such a thing were possible, in the early 21st century than it was in the early 1900s.

What did women's franchise achieve? Emmeline Pankhurst used to say that women's franchise would have three functions: *first of all, a symbol, secondly a safeguard, and thirdly an instrument.* It would be a symbol of what women had achieved, a safeguard against freedom being taken from them and an instrument of social progress.[169] The first two claims were justified by later events, but the granting of the vote to women did not inaugurate the era

of liberal social progress and political probity Emmeline proph-
esied. Indeed, the period immediately after the vote becoming
available to all women, the 1930s, was the most shameful in
modern British politics. The Labour party betrayed its supporters
and the Conservatives received the highest proportion of the vote
they had ever gathered, to dominate governments characterised
by indifference to the poor at home and obeisance to dictators
abroad. Women voters can hardly be held responsible for that,
but they exerted no dramatic positive influence either. Nor were
women voters willing or perhaps able to force 'women's issues'
onto the political agenda. It took 13 elections after 1918 before
the Equal Pay Act was passed. Despite Emmeline's predictions,
definitions of sex crime and legislation over sexual experiences
have continued to be a problem, regardless of a female electorate,
and such issues as the legalisation of prostitution are as controversial as ever.

In those areas of life where anti-suffragists had said women
could not perform, however, they were proved wrong: Margaret
Thatcher was an effective war leader and a tough diplomat. Her
premiership was not, however, distinguished by the sensitivity of
its social policies.

That women must have the vote was fair and just, but the
notion that this might make politics a more fair and just trade
was fanciful. Politics is a profession of promise and betrayal; the
gender of its practitioners is irrelevant.

Emmeline's increasingly backward-looking and strident
emphasis on sexual morality does little for her reputation.
Emmeline's oft-repeated argument that giving women the vote
would solve problems like the (largely imaginary) white slave
trade and child sexual abuse was eccentric and naïve. Emmeline's
answer to the moral double standard between the sexes, Chastity
for Men, was deeply rooted in her own narrow expectations of
female behaviour. She wanted men to become chaste, just as

middle class Victorian women were expected to be, but she failed to recognise that women's limited sexual expression was the result of precisely the social controls against which she was fighting on other fronts. Sexual and political freedoms are entwined. More profound thinkers contemporary with Emmeline strove instead to end the moral double standard by calling for greater sexual freedom for women. Among them were the former WSPU activists Dora Marsden and Mary Gawthorpe and the hundreds of women who came to the discussion circles set up by their magazine *The Freewoman*; and the members of the Legitimation League with their publication *The Adult: The Journal of Sex* proclaiming 'the equal sex freedom of man and woman.'[170]

Emmeline's post-1914 attitudes do stand the test of time, however. In the post Cold War world her anti-Bolshevism does not seem so retrograde. Emmeline's social hygiene lecturing was backward-looking in portraying the sexuality of males as actively guilty and females as passively innocent; but it was forward-looking in its willingness to talk in public about sex.

Emmeline's best contribution as a political leader of the WSPU was, paradoxically, her willingness to step back and allow others to make it work. In five years she took the Union's gatherings from a handful of people meeting in her front room to one of the largest ever meetings in Hyde Park. Yet Emmeline had little to do with the practical details of the organisation that achieved this. More than any others, the Pethick Lawrences were responsible for the nitty-gritty of building the Union into one of the largest political organisations in the country. Emmeline was at her best in her gruelling round of public appearances across Britain.

Emmeline's interventions into the running of the WSPU were less happy. Although expelling the democrats in 1907 was unpopular, the Union did well enough without them. Expelling the Pethick Lawrences in 1912 was a serious blow, however, as the

WSPU thus lost its skilled administrators. Handing control to Christabel, whose skills lay in political strategy rather than day-to-day management, compounded the error.

Emmeline made a great error in allowing her elder daughter to command the movement, while under-using and isolating Adela and marginalising Sylvia. Christabel simply did not show the strength of character of her mother or of many other suffragettes, and while Emmeline was visibly and inspirationally facing injury and death, Christabel was an excellent example of the general who leads from the rear. In failing to see the faults of her offspring, however, Emmeline was hardly remarkable as a

The unveiling of the memorial to Emmeline in Victoria Tower Gardens, London, on 6 March 1930

mother, nor the only leader who has made political errors because of it. Indira Gandhi, a leader much in the mould of Emmeline, doted on her crude and greedy son Sanjay at immense cost to her leadership.[171]

Like many great leaders, in her personal relationships Emmeline Pankhurst does not bear close examination – her qualities are best seen at a distance, where they are truly inspirational. Those inspired by her did not wait until long after death for her public memorial: a statue of her was put up in Victoria Tower Gardens, near the Houses of Parliament, on 6 March 1930. The keynote speaker, Conservative leader Stanley Baldwin, showed his statesman's ability to capture the moment when he said: 'Mrs Pankhurst did not make, nor did she claim to make or to have been the creator of the women's movement . . . But if Mrs Pankhurst did not make the movement, it was she who set the heather on fire.'[172]

Notes:

1   Pankhurst, Sylvia, *The Life of Emmeline Pankhurst* (London 1935) p 125.

2   Pugh, Martin, *The Pankhursts* (London 2001) p 312.

3   Pankhurst, Emmeline, *My Own Story* (London 1979) p 5-6.

4   Pankhurst, *Life*, p 13.

5   Pankhurst, Christabel, *Unshackled: The Story of How We Won the Vote* (London 1959) p 22.

6   Pankhurst, Sylvia, *The Suffragette Movement* (London 1931) p 56.

7   Pankhurst, *Unshackled*, p 21.

8   Pankhurst, *Suffragette Movement*, p 57.

9   Pankhurst, *Suffragette Movement*, p 64.

10   Pankhurst, *Unshackled*, p 27.

11   Pankhurst, *My Own Story*, p 12.

12   Pankhurst, *Unshackled*, p 15.

13   Pankhurst, *Life*, p 23.

14   Pankhurst, *Unshackled*, p 30.

15   *The Times*, 27 April 1892, p 9.

16   Pankhurst, *Suffragette Movement*, p 59.

17   Pankhurst, *Suffragette Movement*, p 103.

18   Pankhurst, *Suffragette Movement*, p 132.

19   Pankhurst, *My Own Story*, p 28.

20   Pankhurst, *Suffragette Movement*, p 136.

21   Pankhurst, *Suffragette Movement,* p 137

22   Benn, Caroline, *Keir Hardie* (London 1992) p 133.

23   Pankhurst, *Life*, p 40. Pankhurst, *Suffragette Movement*, p 147.

24   Pankhurst, *Unshackled*, p 35.

25   Pankhurst, *My Own Story*, p 32.

26   Butler, D and Butler, G, *British Political Facts* (London 1986) p 246.

27   Pankhurst, *Suffragette Movement*, p 168. Pankhurst, *Unshackled*, p 43.

28   Pankhurst, *My Own Story*, p 38.

29   Billington-Greig, Teresa, *The Non-Violent Militant: Selected Writings*, edited by Carol McPhee and Ann Fitzgerald (London 1987) pp 90-1.

30   Benn, Caroline, *Keir Hardie* (London 1992) p 198.

31   Pankhurst, *Suffragette Movement*, p 181.

32   Pankhurst, *Suffragette Movement*, p 217.

33   Pankhurst, *Suffragette Movement*, p 126.

34   Benn, Caroline, *Keir Hardie* (London 1992) p 225.

35   *Hansard*, 12 May 1905, p 233.

36   Pankhurst, *My Own Story*, p 43.

37   Pankhurst, *My Own Story*, p 49.

38   Pugh, *Pankhursts*, p 129.

39   Pankhurst, *My Own Story*, p 49.

40   Pankhurst, *Unshackled*, p 52.

41   Pankhurst, *Suffragette Movement*, p 199.

42   Pankhurst, *My Own Story*, p 56.

43   Pankhurst, *Suffragette Movement*, p 180.

44   Pugh, *Pankhursts*, p 138.

45   Pankhurst, *Suffragette Movement*, p 216.

46   Pethick Lawrence, Frederick, *Fate Has Been Kind* (London 1943) p 73.

47   Pugh, *Pankhursts*, p 154.

48   Pethick Lawrence, Emmeline, *My Part in a Changing World* (London 1938) p 176.

49   Billington-Greig, *The Non-Violent Militant*, p 169.

50   Pethick Lawrence, *Fate Has Been Kind*, p 75.

51   Billington-Greig, *The Non-Violent Militant*, p 171. Figures for membership from Pugh, *Pankhursts,* p 167.

52   Pankhurst, *Suffragette Movement*, p 264.

53   Pankhurst, *My Own Story*, p 59.

54   WSPU pamphlet of 1908, *The Importance of the Vote*.

55   Pankhurst, *Life*, p 72.

56   Pankhurst, *My Own Story*, p 93.

57   Pankhurst, *My Own Story*, p 101.

58   *Votes for Women*, April 1908, p 112.

59   *Hansard*, 28 February 1908, pp 242-4.

60   Pankhurst, *Unshackled*, p 112; *Votes for Women*, 29 October 1908, p 82.

61   Pankhurst, *Suffragette Movement*, p 272.

62   Bartley, Paula, *Emmeline Pankhurst* (London 2002) p 77.

63   Romero, Patricia C E, *Sylvia Pankhurst: Portrait of Radical* (London 1987) p 49.

64   Pankhurst, *Unshackled*, p 130.

65   Pankhurst, *My Own Story*, p 149.

66   Pankhurst, *Suffragette Movement*, p 320.

67   Pankhurst, *Life*, p 94.

68   Pankhurst, *My Own Story*, p 160.

69   Pankhurst, *Suffragette Movement*, p 321.

70   Pankhurst, *Suffragette Movement*, p 323.

71   Pankhurst, *Suffragette Movement*, p 324.

72   Pankhurst, *Unshackled*, p 164.

73   Pankhurst, *My Own Story*, pp 179-80.

74   Pankhurst, *My Own Story*, p 183.

75   Raeburn, Antonia, *The Militant Suffragettes* (London 1973) p 157.

76   Pankhurst, *Life*, p 98.

77   Pankhurst, *My Own Story*, p 199.

78   Pankhurst, *Life*, p 101.

79   Pankhurst, *My Own Story*, p 212.

80   Billington-Greig, *The Non-Violent Militant*, pp 191, 210-11.

81   Billington-Greig, *The Non-Violent Militant*, p 181.

82   St John, Christopher, *Ethel Smyth: A Biography* (London 1959) p 146.

83   Pugh, *Pankhursts*, p 214.

84   Pugh, *Pankhursts*, p 215.

85   Raeburn, *Militant Suffragettes*, p 169.

86   Raeburn, *Militant Suffragettes*, p 167.

87   Pugh, *Pankhursts*, p 226.

88   Pankhurst, *My Own Story*, p 252.

89   Pankhurst, *Life*, p 110.

90   Pethick Lawrence, *Fate Has Been Kind*, p 97.

91   Pankhurst, *Suffragette Movement*, p 406.

92   Pethick Lawrence, *Changing World*, p 277.

93   Pethick Lawrence, *Fate Has Been Kind*, p 99.

94   Pankhurst, *Life*, p 111.

95   Pethick Lawrence, *Changing World*, p 280.
96   Pethick Lawrence, *Changing World*, p 280.
97   Pethick Lawrence, *Fate Has Been Kind*, p 100.
98   Pethick Lawrence, *Changing World*, p 285.
99   Pethick Lawrence, *Fate Has Been Kind*, p 100.
100   *The Suffragette*, 25 October 1912, p 16; Pankhurst, *My Own Story*, p 266.
101   *Votes for Women*, 16 August 1912, p 749.
102   Benn, *Keir Hardie*, p 315.
103   Pankhurst, *Suffragette Movement*, p 401.
104   Pankhurst, *Suffragette Movement*, p 396.
105   Pankhurst, *My Own Story*, p 261.
106   Pankhurst, *Suffragette Movement*, p 401.
107   *The Suffragette*, 28 February 1913, p 309.
108   *The Suffragette*, 25 October 1912, p 16.
109   *The Suffragette*, 11 April 1913, p 422.
110   Pankhurst, *Suffragette Movement*, p 401.
111   Smyth, Ethel, *Female Pipings in Eden* (London 1934) p 213.
112   Smyth, *Female Pipings*, p 214.
113   Smyth, *Female Pipings*, p 214.
114   Pankhurst, *Suffragette Movement*, p 328.
115   Raeburn, *Militant Suffragettes*, p 174.
116   *The Suffragette*, 13 June 1913, p 580.
117   Fulford, Roger, *Votes for Women* (London 1958) p 252.
118   Pankhurst, *Suffragette Movement*, p 469.
119   Pankhurst, *Unshackled*, p 254.
120   Smyth, *Female Pipings*, p 218.
121   Stansgate, Lady, *My Exit Visa* (London 1992); interview with author 15 June 1989.
122   *The Suffragette*, 18 July 1913, p 677.
123   Smyth, *Female Pipings*, pp 225, 230.
124   Pankhurst, *Suffragette Movement*, p 491.
125   Pankhurst, *Suffragette Movement*, p 491.
126   Purvis, June, *Emmeline Pankhurst: A Biography* (London 2002) p 239.
127   Pankhurst, *Suffragette Movement*, p 517.
128   Benn, *Keir Hardie*, p 312.

129   Pankhurst, *Suffragette Movement*, p 521.

130   Billington-Greig, Teresa, 'The Truth About White Slavery' in *Englishwoman's Review*, June 1913, p 445.

131   Purvis, *Emmeline Pankhurst,* p 237.

132   Pethick Lawrence, *Fate Has Been Kind*, p 68.

133   Smyth, *Female Pipings*, p 233.

134   *The Suffragette*, 13 March 1914, p 492.

135   Raeburn, *Militant Suffragettes*, p 225.

136   *The Times*, 11 March 1914, p 9.

137   Pankhurst, *Suffragette Movement*, p 544.

138   Pankhurst, *Life*, p 307.

139   Pankhurst, *My Own Story,* p 334.

140   Raeburn, *Militant Suffragettes*, p 231.

141   Pankhurst, *Life*, p 144.

142   Raeburn, *Militant Suffragettes*, p 232. *The Suffragette*, 29 May 1914, p 120.

143   Romero, *Sylvia Pankhurst,* p 83.

144   Pankhurst, *Suffragette Movement*, p 570.

145   Pankhurst, *Suffragette Movement*, p 575.

146   *The Times*, 8 July 1914, p 10.

147   *The Suffragette*, 7 August 1914, p 301.

148   Pugh, *Pankhursts*, p 300

149   Pankhurst, *Life*, p 153.

150   Pankhurst, *Suffragette Movement*, p 595.

151   Smyth, *Female Pipings*, p 230.

152   Purvis, *Emmeline Pankhurst*, p 269.

153   Smyth, *Female Pipings*, p 238.

154   Smyth, *Female Pipings*, p 241.

155   *The Suffragette*, 28 May 1915, p 111.

156   Lloyd George, D, *War Memoirs*, Vol ii (London 1933) p 1172.

157   Craigie, Jill, introduction to Pankhurst, *My Own Story*, no page numbers.

158   Smyth, *Female Pipings*, p 259.

159   Pugh, *Pankhursts*, p 335.

160   *Britannia*, 8 November 1918, p 188.

161   *Britannia*, 22 November 1918, p 203.

162   *The Times*, 20 November 1918, p10.

163   Smyth, *Female Pipings*, p 246.

164   Pankhurst, *Life*, p 173.

165   Smyth, *Female Pipings*, p 269 of 1933 edition – deleted from following edition.

166   Pethick Lawrence, *Changing World*, p 284.

167   Pankhurst, *Suffragette Movement*, p 512.

168   Pankhurst, *Unshackled*, p 119.

169   Pankhurst, Emmeline, *Importance of the Vote*, text of a lecture delivered at the Portman Rooms, 24 March 1908, published by WSPU.

170   Bland, Lucy, *Banishing the Beast: Sexuality and the Early Feminists* (New York 1995) pp 156-7, 265-9.

171   Adams, J and Whitehead, P, *The Dynasty: The Nehru–Gandhi Story* (London 1997) pp 246-66.

172   Smyth, *Female Pipings*, p 276.

Chronology

Year	History	Culture
1858	Treaty of Tientsin ends Anglo-Chinese War. Powers of the East India Company are transferred to the British Crown.	George Eliot, *Adam Bede*.
1870	Franco-Prussian War. Papal Rome annexed by Italy. In US, John Rockefeller founds Standard Oil.	Clément Delibes, *Coppélia*. Dostoevsky, *The House of the Dead*.
1872	In Philippines, rebellion against Spain.	Thomas Hardy, *Under the Greenwood Tree*.
1872	First International Association football match, England versus Scotland.	
1876	China declares Korea an independent state. Turkish massacre of Bulgarians. Battle of Little Bighorn; General Custer dies. Alexander Graham Bell invents telephone.	Johannes Brahms, *First Symphony*. Wagner, *Siegfried*. First complete performance of Wagner's *The Ring*.
1878	Congress of Berlin resolves Balkan crisis. Serbia becomes independent. Britain gains Cyprus. Second Anglo-Afghan War (until 1879). In London, electric street lighting.	Tchaikovsky, *Swan Lake*.
1879	Germany and Austria-Hungary form Dual Alliance. In Africa, Zulu War. In south Africa, Boers proclaim Transvaal Republic. In South America, War of the Pacific (until 1883).	Anton Bruckner, Sixth Symphony. Tchaikovsky, *Eugene Onegin*. Ibsen, *The Doll's House*. August Strindberg, *The Red Room*.
1880	In Britain, William Gladstone becomes prime minister. First Boer War (until 1881). Louis Pasteur discovers streptococcus.	Tchaikovsky, *1812 Overture*. Dostoevsky, *The Brothers Karamazov*.
1882	Phoenix Park murders, Dublin.	Édouard Manet, *Bar at the Folies Bergères*.
1883	Jewish immigration to Palestine (Rothschild Colonies). Germany acquires southwest Africa. In Chicago, world's first skyscraper built.	Antonín Dvořák, *Stabat Mater*. Robert Louis Stevenson, *Treasure Island*.

1884   27 February: Francis Henry (Frank) born.

1885   They leave the Goulden family house while Emmeline is pregnant with Adela. 19 June: Adela born. Richard unsuccessfully stands as a Radical parliamentary candidate in Rotherhithe, south-east London. Emmeline opens a shop, Emerson & Co, on Hampstead Road, London.

1888   11 September: death of Frank.

1889   Family lives in Russell Square where Emmeline hosts political soirées. Emersons moves to Berners Street. 7 July: Henry Francis (Harry) born. Shortly after the birth, the Women's Franchise League is founded.

1892   April: Emmeline and members of the WFL disrupt a meeting in support of a single-women's franchise bill.

1893   Family return to Manchester amid financial problems. Emersons fails. Emmeline joins the Independent Labour Party and soon after leaves the Liberals.

1894   December: Emmeline elected to Chorlton Board of Guardians of the Poor Law.

1895   July: Richard stands unsuccessfully as a parliamentary candidate for the ILP for Gorton.

1884	Sino-French War (until 1885). Berlin Conference to mediate European claims in Africa (until 1885). In Mexico, Porfirio Diaz becomes president (until 1911).	Jules Massenet, *Manon*. Mark Twain, *Huckleberry Finn*. Georges Seurat, *Une Baignade, Asnières*.
1885	Belgium's King Leopold II establishes Independent Congo State. In Transvaal, gold discovered. Gottlieb Daimler invents prototype of motorcycle.	Zola, *Germinal*. Guy de Maupassant, *Bel Ami*.
1888	In Germany, William II becomes emperor (until 1918). In Asia, French Indo-China established. In Brazil, slavery abolished.	N Rimsky-Korsakov, *Scheherezade* (op 35). Edward Bellamy, *Looking Backwards*. Rudyard Kipling, *Plain Tales from the Hills*. Strindberg, *Miss Julie*. George Eastman invents the first commercial roll-film camera: the 'Kodak' box.
1889	Second Socialist International. Italy invades Somalia and Ethiopia. In Paris, Eiffel Tower completed. Brazil proclaims itself a republic.	Richard Strauss, *Don Juan*. Verdi, *Falstaff*. George Bernard Shaw, *Fabian Essays*.
1892	Gladstone's *Fourth Ministry*	Maurice Maeterlinck, *Pelléas et Mélisande*
1893	Franco-Russian alliance signed. South Africa Company launches Matabele War. France annexes Laos.	Dvořák, *From the New World*. Tchaikovsky, *Pathétique*. Wilde, *A Woman of No Importance*.
1894	In France, President Carnot assassinated. Uganda becomes British protectorate. In France, Alfred Dreyfus convicted of treason. In Russia, Nicholas II becomes tsar (until 1917). Sino-Japanese War (until 1895). In US, Pullman strike.	Claude Debussy, *L'Après-midi d'un Faune*. Gabriele d'Annuzio, *Il trionfo della morte*. Kipling, *The Jungle Book*. G B Shaw, *Arms and Man*.
1895	In Britain, Lord Salisbury becomes prime minister. Cuban rebellion begins. Japan conquers Taiwan (Formosa). Lumière brothers invent the cinematograph. Guglielmo Marconi invents wireless telegraphy. Wilhelm Röntgen invents X-rays.	H G Wells, *The Time Machine*. W B Yeats, *Poems*. Wilde, *The Importance of Being Earnest*.

1896   Free speech agitation over Boggart Hole Clough. Emmeline appears in court from June.

1898   Emmeline elected to the National Administrative Council of the ILP. June: Emmeline and Christabel travel to Geneva. 4 July: Death of Richard Pankhurst aged 58. Family moves to Nelson Street. Emmeline again opens a shop, Emersons, and begins to work as a Registrar.

1900   November: Emmeline successfully stands as ILP candidate for Manchester School Board.

1903   10 October: Founding of Women's Social and Political Union.

1905   12 May: Women's Enfranchisement Bill, on which Emmeline and Keir Hardie have worked for months, is talked out. Emmeline spontaneously holds her first demonstration at the Houses of Parliament. 13 October: Christabel and Annie Kenney are arrested and imprisoned for disrupting a Liberal meeting by calling for votes for women. Emmeline organises demonstrations in their support and release celebrations.

1906   19 February: Emmeline, addressing supporters at Caxton Hall, calls for immediate march to lobby Parliament when the King's Speech omits mention of votes for women. April: Emmeline and other suffrage leaders see the Prime Minister: no hope of action in the near future. Emmeline launches policy of harassing ministers. Emersons finally closes. October: Emmeline thrown to the floor of the House of Commons lobby in a confused rush. Eleven women arrested.

1907   Emmeline and Christabel resign from the ILP. 13 February: 'Prison volunteers' women's parliament at Caxton Hall. Five hours of battle with police. Emmeline resigns as Registrar, becomes a full-time speaker for the WSPU. Now continuously on the move from one by-election to another, opposing government candidates. September: Emmeline tears up WSPU constitution. Departure of Teresa Billington, Charlotte Despard and other activists who called for a democratic organisation.

1908   7 January: Emmeline seriously attacked by thugs at Newton Abbot by-election. February: Emmeline addresses 100,000 people on Hunslet Moor for the South Leeds by-election. Returns on 13 February to lead a deputation to petition Parliament and is arrested for the first time. First imprisonment: six weeks. 19 March: On the same day she is released from prison, Emmeline addresses Albert Hall meeting, the largest ever indoor suffrage gathering. April: Herbert Asquith, principal opponent of women's suffrage, becomes Prime Minister. 21 June: Women's Day in Hyde Park. Up to half a million people attend the Union's largest ever demonstration. 30 June: Stone throwers break Prime Minister's windows during demonstration outside Parliament, Emmeline approves of their

1896	Theodore Herzl founds Zionism.	Giacomo Puccini, *La Bohème*.

1896	Theodore Herzl founds Zionism. First Olympic Games of the modern era held in Athens. Antoine (Henri) Becquerel discovers radioactivity of uranium.	Giacomo Puccini, *La Bohème*. Thomas Hardy, *Jude the Obscure*.
1898	Spanish-American War: Spain loses Cuba, Puerto Rico and the Philippines. Britain conquers Sudan.	Henry James, *The Turn of the Screw*. H G Wells, *The War of the Worlds*. Zola, *J'Accuse*. Auguste Rodin, *The Kiss*.
1900	First Pan-African Conference. In France, Dreyfus pardoned. Relief of Mafeking. In China, Boxer Rebellion (until 1901). Aspirin introduced. First Zeppelin flight.	Puccini, *Tosca*. Conrad, *Lord Jim*. Sigmund Freud, *The Interpretation of Dreams*.
1903	Bolshevik–Menshevik split in Communist Party of Russia. In Russia, pogroms against Jews. In Britain, suffragette movement begins. Panama Canal Zone granted to US to build and manage waterway. Wright Brothers' first flight.	Henry James, *The Ambassadors*.
1905	Russian revolution against monarchy fails. Bloody Sunday massacre. Korea becomes protectorate of Japan.	Richard Strauss, *Salome*. Albert Einstein, *Special Theory of Relativity*. Paul Cézanne, *Les Grandes Baigneuses*.
1906	Algeciras Conference resolves dispute between France and Germany over Morocco. Duma created in Russia. Revolution in Iran.	Henri Matisse, *Bonheur de vivre*. Maxim Gorky, *The Mother* (until 1907).
1907	Anglo-Russian Entente. Electric washing-machine invented.	Conrad, *The Secret Agent*. Rainer Maria Rilke, *Neue Gedichte*.
1908	Bulgaria becomes independent. Austria-Hungary annexes Bosnia-Herzegovina.	Gustav Mahler, *Das Lied von der Erde* (until 1909). E M Forster, *A Room with a View*. Cubism begins with Picasso and Braque.

actions. October: Demonstration calling on supporters to 'Rush the House of Commons' leads to incitement to riot charges for Emmeline, Christabel and Flora Drummond. Trial is a propaganda triumph for the WSPU. Emmeline sentenced to three months.19 December: Early release to an ecstatic public welcome.

1909   29 June: Emmeline arrested in front of Parliament while trying to exercise the right of petition. She is sentenced but her fine is paid by an anonymous donor. In protest at violence towards demonstrators, government buildings are stoned. July: Marion Wallace Dunlop, in Holloway, hunger strikes and is released. Other women follow the same tactic. September: Forcible feeding starts. October to December: Emmeline on a successful tour of USA and Canada.

1910   5 January: Harry Pankhurst dies. 31 January: Truce in militant activities declared amid hopes that new government will make concessions. High hopes placed on 'Conciliation Bill'. June and July: Widely supported peaceful demonstrations. 18 November: Emmeline calls off truce when government fails to find time for Conciliation Bill. She leads immediate march on Parliament; 'wholesale brutality' of Black Friday. 22 November: Emmeline leads another spontaneous demonstration, to Downing Street. She is arrested but discharged the next day. 25 December: Emmeline's sister, Mary Clarke, dies.

1911   January: Truce renewed with a new parliament and a resurrection of the Conciliation Bill. November: Emmeline is in USA on a second lecture tour when news comes that Asquith has announced a manhood suffrage bill (which will mean the end of the Conciliation Bill). She orders members to protest: widespread smashing of private as well as government windows.

1912   16 February: Emmeline announces 'the argument of the stone'. 1 March: Emmeline breaks windows at Downing Street; widespread window-breaking now and three days later. In all 217 women arrested including Emmeline who receives a two-month sentence. Police raid on WSPU headquarters. May: Emmeline and the Pethick Lawrences are tried at the Old Bailey for conspiracy and sentenced to nine months. June: Emmeline's first hunger strike as part of a mass action in Holloway. 24 June: Emmeline and others released on health grounds. July: Emmeline and Pethick Lawrences meet Christabel in exile in France and disagree over strategy of 'civil war' policy of militancy. 14 October: Pethick Lawrences expelled from the Union. 17 October: Emmeline at the Albert Hall outlines a new policy of extreme militancy, urging attacks on 'the sacred idol of property'.

1913   January: The Speaker rules against a women's amendment to the manhood suffrage bill. The bill is dropped. Arson and sabotage escalate. Emmeline never repudiates any militant action: 'I want to be tried for sedition.' 24 February: Emmeline arrested in connection with the bombing of Lloyd George's house five days earlier. April: Emmeline sentenced to three years at the Old Bailey. Bomb and arson attacks throughout the country. Emmeline goes on hunger strike in Holloway. 12 April: Emmeline released under terms to be enshrined in the new Cat and Mouse Act, to be re-arrested when she is stronger. Altogether she is re-arrested nine times, hunger striking at each imprisonment. 4 June: Emily Wilding Davison dies under the hoofs of horses while demonstrating at Epsom.

1909	In Britain, pensions begin.	Strauss, *Elektra*.

1909   In Britain, pensions begin.
        In Britain, Lloyd George's 'People's
        Budget' is rejected by House of Lords;
        causes constitutional crisis.
        Congo Free State under direct rule by
        Belgian parliament.
        In Turkey, Young Turk revolution.
        In Nicaragua, US supports revolution.
        In Britain, Girl Guide movement founded.
        Pope Pius X beatifies Joan of Arc.
        Henry Ford introduces Model T car.

        Strauss, *Elektra*.
        Rabindranath Tagore, *Gitanjali*.
        Sergey Diaghilev forms Les Ballets
        Russes.
        F T Marinetto publishes manifesto
        of futurism in *Le Figaro*.

1910   George V becomes king of Britain.
        Union of South Africa created.
        Japan annexes Korea.

        Constantin Brancusi, *La Muse
        endormie*.
        Igor Stravinsky, *The Firebird*.
        Forster, *Howard's End*.
        Bertrand Russell, *Principia mathe-
        matica*.
        Post-impressionist exhibition,
        London.

1911   In Britain, Parliament Act resolves consti-
        tutional crisis.
        In Britain, National Insurance to provide
        sickness benefits begins.
        Chinese revolution against imperial dynasties.
        Roald Amundsen reaches South Pole.
        Ernest Rutherford discovers the nuclear
        model of the atom.

        Stravinsky, *Der Rosenkavalier*.

1912   Balkan Wars (until 1913).
        ANC formed in South Africa.
        Titanic sinks.
        Morocco becomes French protectorate.
        Dr Sun Yat-sen establishes Republic of
        China.
        Stainless steel invented.

        Arnold Schoenberg, *Pierrot lunaire*.
        Carl Jung, *The Psychology of the
        Unconscious*.
        Bertrand Russell, *The Problems of
        Philosophy*.

1913   In US, Woodrow Wilson becomes presi-
        dent (until 1921).
        In Greece, George I assassinated.
        In China, rebellion in Yangzi Valley.
        In China, Yuan Shikai elected president.
        Hans Geiger invents Geiger counter.

        Stravinsky, *The Rite of Spring*.
        Guillaume Apollinaire, *Les peintres
        cubistes*.
        D H Lawrence, *Sons and Lovers*.
        Marcel Proust, *A la recherche du
        temps perdu* (until 1927).

14 June: Emmeline arrested on the morning of Davison's funeral. October and November: American tour. Emmeline is arrested on return before landing.

1914   January: Emmeline and Christabel expel Sylvia from the WSPU and send Adela to Australia. 9 March: Violent arrest of Emmeline in Glasgow. Widespread protest including slashing of the Rokeby Venus. 21 May: Re-arrest of Emmeline outside Buckingham Palace during major demonstration. August: Emmeline orders supporters to suspend all activity until the international crisis is over. Home Secretary releases all suffragette prisoners unconditionally on August 10. September: Emmeline begins patriotic appeals for men to fight and women to do war work.

1915   June: Emmeline adopts four 'war babies'. 17 July: Emmeline leads demonstration for women to do work in munitions and other formerly male jobs.

1917   Emmeline refuses to join with suffragists in making recommendations for the Electoral Reform Bill. June to October: Emmeline in Russia to boost resolve for the war. 2 November: WSPU relaunched as the Women's Party. December: Electoral Reform Bill passes the House of Commons, giving women over 30 the vote on a property qualification.

1918   June: Emmeline travels to North America to urge international intervention in Russia to bring down the Bolsheviks. 14 December: Christabel stands unsuccessfully as Women's Party candidate for Smethwick.

1919   September: Emmeline leaves for five years in North America where she lectures on anti-Bolshevism and 'social hygiene'.

1914	28 June: Archduke Franz Ferdinand assassinated in Sarajevo. First World War begins. Panama Canal opens. Egypt becomes British protectorate.	James Joyce, *The Dubliners*. Ezra Pound, *Des Imagistes*.
1915	Dardanelles/Gallipoli campaign (until 1916). Italy denounces its Triple Alliance with Germany and Austria-Hungary. In Britain, Herbert Asquith forms coalition government. In Brussels, Germans execute Edith Cavell. In Britain, Women's Institute founded. In US, William J Simmons revives the Ku Klux Klan. Albert Einstein introduces general theory of relativity.	John Buchan, *The Thirty-Nine Steps*. D H Lawrence, *The Rainbow*. Ezra Pound, *Cathay*. Marcel Duchamp, *The Large Glass* or *The Bride Stripped Bare by her Bachelors, Even* (until 1923). Pablo Picasso, *Harlequin*.
1917	In Russia, revolutions in February and October. Tsar Nicholas II abdicates. Communists seize power under Vladimir Lenin. Battle of Passchendaele. US enters First World War. British take Baghdad. Balfour Declaration on Palestine: Britain favours creation of Jewish state without prejudice to non-Jewish communities.	First recording of New Orleans jazz. Franz Kafka, *Metamorphosis*. T S Eliot, *Prufrock and Other Observations*. Giorgio de Chirico, *Le Grand Métaphysique*.
1918	Treaty of Brest-Litovsk between Russia and the Central Powers. In Russia, Tsar Nicholas II and family executed. 11 November: Armistice agreement ends First World War. British take Palestine and Syria. In UK, women over 30 get right to vote. In UK, food shortage leads to establishment of National Food Kitchens and rationing; prime minister appeals to women to help with the harvest. 'Spanish flu' epidemic kills at least 20m people in Europe, US and India.	Oswald Spengler, *The Decline of the West*, Volume 1. Amédée Ozenfant and Le Corbusier, *Après le Cubisme*. Paul Klee, *Gartenplan*.
1919	Treaty of Versailles. Spartacist revolt in Germany. Poland, Hungary, Czechoslovakia, Estonia, Lithuania and Latvia become republics. Comintern held in Moscow. In US, prohibition begins. Irish Civil War (until 1921).	Franz Kafka, *In the Penal Colony*. J M Keynes, *The Economic Consequences of the Peace*. United Artists formed with Charlie Chaplin, Mary Pickford, Douglas Fairbanks and D W Griffith as partners.

1924   Stays in Bermuda.

1925   Unsuccessfully runs a tea shop in Juan-les-Pins, France. Returns to Britain.

1926   December: Adopted as Conservative parliamentary candidate in Whitechapel in London's East End.

1927   4 December: Sylvia gives birth to Richard Keir Pethick Pankhurst.

1928   March: Women given the vote on equal terms with men. 14 June: Emmeline dies, aged 69, in a nursing home on Wimpole Street, London.

1924	Vladimir Lenin dies.	Forster, *A Passage to India*. Kafka, *The Hunger Artist*. Thomas Mann, *The Magic Mountain*. André Breton, first surrealist manifesto.
1925	Pact of Locarno. Chiang Kai-shek launches campaign to unify China. Discovery of ionosphere.	Erik Satie dies. F Scott Fitzgerald, *The Great Gatsby*. Kafka, *The Trial*. Adolf Hitler, *Mein Kampf* (Vol. 1). Sergey Eisenstein, *Battleship Potemkin*. Television invented.
1926	Germany joins League of Nations. Antonio Gramsci imprisoned in Italy. France establishes Republic of Lebanon. Hirohito becomes emperor of Japan.	Puccini, *Turandot*. Kafka, *The Castle*. T E Lawrence, *The Seven Pillars of Wisdom*. A A Milne, *Winnie the Pooh*. Fritz Lang, *Metropolis*.
1927	Joseph Stalin comes to power. Charles Lindbergh flies across Atlantic.	Martin Heidegger, *Being and Time*. Virginia Woolf, *To the Lighthouse*. BBC public radio launched.
1928	Kellogg-Briand Pact for Peace. Alexander Fleming discovers penicillin.	Maurice Ravel, *Boléro*. Kurt Weill, *The Threepenny Opera*. Huxley, *Point Counter Point*. D H Lawrence, *Lady Chatterley's Lover*. W B Yeats, *The Tower*. Walt Disney, *Steamboat Willie*.

Further Reading

Select Bibliography

Any reader of works about Emmeline Pankhurst must tread carefully: she stimulated controversy no less after her life than during it. Her central position in the movement meant she stood on several fault lines: militants against non-militants; destructive militants against demonstrative militants; socialists against conservatives; feminist suffragists against universal suffragists; and she occupied different roles herself at different times.

Work by the primary participants must take precedence over secondary sources but it is as well to remember that secondary writers are normally at least making some attempt at impartiality. There is no such constraint on the Pankhursts, whose family quarrels have long outlived them.

Books by participants in the events:

Billington-Greig, Teresa, *The Non-Violent Militant: Selected Writings,* edited by Carol McPhee and Ann Fitzgerald (London 1987): collection of writings by one of the sharpest suffragette minds, who unfortunately did not complete her own history of the movement, having failed to find a publisher.

Billington-Greig, Teresa, *The Truth About White Slavery* in *Englishwoman's Review*, June 1913: devastating critique of Emmeline and Christabel's 'white slavery' beliefs.

Pankhurst, E Sylvia, *The Suffragette Movement* (London 1931): a considerable updating of her 1911 text *The Suffragette*. The most complete version of events and picture of personalities as well as being a classic of autobiography; but from the perspective of a daughter who was marginalised then expelled from the movement.

Pankhurst, E Sylvia, *The Life of Emmeline Pankhurst* (London 1935): accurate and informative but repeats much of the material in the above.

Pankhurst, Christabel, *Unshackled: The Story of How We Won the Vote* (London 1959, but written in the 1930s after her sister's version had been published): a bald factual account omitting many of the events which Sylvia considered essential – such as the expulsion of Sylvia.

Pankhurst, Emmeline, *My Own Story* (London 1979, introduction by Jill Craigie): text written by an American journalist from extended conversations with Emmeline Pankhurst and newspaper clippings. Often inaccurate as history but an excellent representation of Emmeline's vivid patterns of speech.

Pethick Lawrence, Frederick, *Fate Has Been Kind* (London 1943); and Pethick Lawrence, Emmeline, *My Part in a Changing World* (London 1938): autobiographies of these active radicals with good descriptions of Emmeline Pankhurst and their work in the WSPU.

Smyth, Ethel, *Female Pipings in Eden* (London 1933 and 1934 – revised version which omits some of the more sensitive material): an affectionate memoir of Emmeline by a close friend.

Strachey, Ray, *The Cause: A Short History of the Women's Movement in Great Britain* (London 1928): the suffrage campaign from the point of view of the National Union of Women's Suffrage Societies.

Secondary sources:

Bartley, Paula, *Emmeline Pankhurst* (London 2002): biography emphasising continuity in Emmeline's behaviour.

Benn, Caroline, *Keir Hardie* (London 1992): definitive biography of the radical socialist.

Bland, Lucy, *Banishing the Beast: Sexuality and the Early Feminists* (New York 1995): analysis of how 'social purity' penetrated feminist thinking in the nineteenth and early twentieth centuries.

Fulford, Roger, *Votes for Women* (London 1958): irreverent history of the women's suffrage campaign from its earliest days.

Liddington, Jill and Norris, Jill, *One Hand Tied Behind Us* (London 1978): on northern, working-class suffragists.

Lloyd, Trevor, *Suffragettes International* (London 1971): brief appraisal of suffrage reform around the world.

Marcus, Jane, *Suffrage and the Pankhursts* (London 1987): collection of texts by the Pankhursts with an introductory essay.

Pugh, Martin, *The Pankhursts* (London 2001): thorough telling of the whole Pankhurst family psychodrama in its political context.

Purvis, June, *Emmeline Pankhurst: A Biography* (London 2002): comprehensively researched biography viewing Emmeline from a feminist perspective.

Raeburn, Antonia, *The Militant Suffragettes* (London 1973): detailed account of the WSPU's activities concentrating on militancy.

Romero, Patricia C E, *Sylvia Pankhurst: Portrait of a Radical* (London 1987): somewhat critical biography of the most rebellious Pankhurst.

Stanley, Liz with Morley, Ann, *The Life and Death of Emily Wilding Davison* (London 1988): life of the famous militant incorporating an earlier biography.

Newspapers

Votes for Women: owned by the Pethick Lawrences, launched in October 1907 and supportive of WSPU alone until October 1912, then generally covering all suffrage campaigning.

The Suffragette: newspaper edited by Christabel Pankhurst. Started in October 1912 when the Pethick Lawrences were expelled (from October 1915 called *Britannia*).

The Women's Library in London is the primary source for suffrage material but research for this book has also taken place in the British Library, University of London Library and the House of Commons Library; thank you to the staff of all these institutions for their assistance. The help of Julie Peakman of the Wellcome Institute/University College London is also appreciated for her valuable comments on the text.

Picture Sources

The author and publishers wish to express their thanks to the following sources of illustrative material and/or permission to reproduce it. They will make the proper acknowledgements in future editions in the event that any omissions have occurred.

Heritage Image Pictures: pp. 10, 21, 34, 42, 59, 64, 66, 73, 80, 84, 85, 87, 90, 94, 104, 117, 128, 132, 138; Mary Evans Picture Library: pp. vi, 7, 8, 13, 76, 82, 156; Topham Picturepoint: pp. i, iii, 24, 36, 37, 38, 67, 103, 106, 121; Ann Ronan Picture Library: pp. 48, 57, 71, 79, 110, 112, 125, 130, 146.

Index

Odyssey, 6
old-age pensions, 39, 71, 79
Oliver Twist (Dickens), 25
Oxted station, 106